contemporary

Classics

contemporary
Classics

Jean Moss

CRE🏠TIVE
HOMEOWNER®

To Ann Banks, the best knitter I know.

First published in North America in 2007 by

CRE▲TIVE
HOMEOWNER®

Upper Saddle River, NJ
Creative Homeowner® is a registered trademark of
Federal Marketing Corporation

Current printing (last digit): 10 9 8 7 6 5 4 3 2 1
Library of Congress Control Number: 2007922563
ISBN 10: 1-58011-367-2
ISBN 13: 978-1-58011-367-0

Senior Editor: Clare Sayer
Production: Marion Storz
Design: Isobel Gillan
Photography: Sian Irvine
Illustrations and charts: Carrie Hill
Editorial Direction: Rosemary Wilkinson

Reproduction by Pica Digital PTE Ltd, Singapore
Printed and bound by Times Offset, Malaysia

CREATIVE HOMEOWNER
A division of Federal Marketing Corp.
24 Park Way
Upper Saddle River
NJ 07458
www.creativehomeowner.com

Contents

Introduction

I was delighted to be asked to design a book of contemporary classics. Today's knitters are often pressed for time, so to create fashionable pieces that will last is an essential part of a designer's brief. After all, who wants to spend time knitting something that will be unwearable within a few months? I invariably reach for my old favorites when pressed because I know they won't let me down. This was instilled into me years ago by Ralph Lauren, who insisted that sweaters should become old friends and get better as the years go by.

The heyday of the elegant woman was the fifties and sixties. This was the era of glamorous actresses such as Grace Kelly, Elizabeth Taylor, Elinor Parker, Katharine Hepburn, and, of course, Audrey Hepburn—each a huge inspiration. However, in *Contemporary Classics* you won't find slavishly reproduced retro knits. My aim was to capture the elusive magic of these icons and knit it into each design. Of course, in setting the scene, there's a nod to the clichés such as Hermes headscarf and large sunglasses, but importantly, I feel the sweaters should also stand alone as chic, simple, and elegant.

Audrey Hepburn's philosophy was, "Wear your clothes, don't let them wear you," and I totally agree. Bearing this in mind, I've designed a versatile collection of sweaters to get you through each day, no matter what the occasion. Initially our clothes define us, so why not make sure the image you present is made up of unique pieces personal to you, rather than the hackneyed offerings of the chain stores? There's an upsurge in the popularity of all things hand-made as people become tired of the homogenous nature of store-bought goods. I'm often asked about the sweaters I wear myself, and sometimes I'm proud to say that they were part of collections I designed twenty years ago. Time is the

test of a true classic, and I know I've succeeded when a vintage piece is admired today.

Knitting is empowering, and *Contemporary Classics* places elegant, stylish, and lasting pieces firmly within the grasp of anyone who can master the basic knit stitch—in, around, over, and off. Add your own special touches—beads, a different edging, play around with the colors and stripes, or simply follow the pattern and you should end up with an original, handcrafted sweater to cherish and be proud of.

To knit is also comforting and relaxing—a way of channeling your creativity and expressing your personality. No two pieces will ever be the same—even from the same pattern, and it's this human element that makes knitting so special. It's been a lifetime's vocation for me to make good design available to everyone who wants it.

Contemporary Classics is full of straightforward patterns, designed to offer new and improving knitters stylish and knittable classics. You won't feel intimidated by complicated intarsia or intricate cables—you need only the basic knit and purl stitches to master most of the designs. My brief was to create sweaters that could be knitted up in three weekends, so even the busiest career girl can find projects to fit her hectic schedule. Many designs can be completed by beginners, while the average knitter will find all the designs within her/his capabilities.

I've taken great care to choose beautiful yarns to complement my designs—being a profligate yarn consumer, I find it nearly impossible to resist the temptation of a sumptuous new fiber. There's never been a more exciting time to visit a yarn shop, and research is going on all the time to fuel the quality yarn experience which today's knitter demands. You can find every possible blend and

composition from traditional wool, alpaca, cashmere, cotton, and silk to the new and innovative yarns made from fibers such as bamboo, soya, and hemp, with many exciting blends in between.

Choosing yarn is a sensual experience—a yarn needs to feel good and look good, and that's why I've always loved natural fibers. However, there are now so many interesting and beautiful man-made fibers that it's not so clear-cut any longer. One of the most thrilling yet challenging jobs of a designer is selecting the perfect yarn for a design. Swatching helps to get the handle right, but it's only when the sweater is knitted that you know for sure that you've made all the right decisions. When a new sweater arrives, knitted by one of my team of studio knitters, I'm like a child at Christmas!

Knitting is soothing and sociable—it connects people. If you're new to the craft, don't be afraid to pick up your needles and go down to your local yarn shop, where you'll find lots of friendly knitters only too pleased to share their knowledge and get you going.

In this collection, I've looked to the effortless elegance of the cinematic icons of the fifties and sixties to create contemporary designs for a new century. Stanley Donen, who directed Audrey Hepburn in *Funny Face*, famously said "Audrey makes my soul fly. She opens me up to beautiful feelings." We could all do with some of that, and I hope that you'll find it in every page of *Contemporary Classics*.

Knit On,

Erin Moss

General information

NEEDLES AND OTHER EQUIPMENT

Just as I wouldn't invest my time knitting with poor quality yarns, I wouldn't use uninspiring accessories. There are so many ways of extending the feel good factor in knitting and beautiful, fun accessories is high on the list. I use Brittany hardwood straight needles, and Addi Turbo circulars, but there are many different types of fabulous needles in the shops. Other accessories that you'll find useful are stitch markers, stitch holders, row counter, knitting needle gauge, tape measure, scissors, glass-headed pins, tapestry sewing needle, point protectors—to stop the knitting from falling off the ends of your needles—and lastly, a knitting bag. This can be anything from a recycled plastic bag to a state-of-the-art tote. Get the best out of your knitting, indulge yourself with a few toys and treats and make it a feast for the eyes from start to finish.

BUTTONS

Never skimp on trimmings, choose them carefully to highlight your sweater, which has taken lots of your valuable time to knit. If you just can't find what you're looking for, make your own using button blanks covered with knitted fabric. Color is important, and if you can't get an exact match to the yarn, then often it's better to go for a complete contrast. Also consider scale when buying buttons. The balance of the sweater will be thrown out of kilter if you get this wrong. If you have a bold design in chunky yarn, you need big buttons to complement it. Weight of yarn is important, too. Buttons need to be up to the job of fastening the garment, and thick yarn will produce holes that will be too large for small buttons. A fine silk yarn looks stunning with mother-of-pearl buttons but will never look elegant with heavy wooden buttons.

KNITTING NEEDLE CONVERSION TABLE

US	METRIC	UK
00	2mm	14
1	2¼mm	13
2	2¾mm	12
2/3	3mm	11
3	3¼mm	10
4	3½mm	
5	3¾mm	9
6	4mm	8
7	4½mm	7
8	5mm	6
9	5½mm	5
10	6mm	4
10½	6½mm	3
11	8mm	0
13	9mm	00
15	10mm	000
17	12mm	
19	15mm	

YARN INFORMATION

I've used favorite yarns from Rowan, Jaeger, Artesano, Debbie Bliss, and Sirdar in this book, all of which are widely available. Each pattern gives details of a particular yarn and it's always best to use that yarn. However, if you can't locate a specific yarn or wish to use yarn from your stash, do substitute it with one with similar yardage. All yardages are listed below.

Artesano Inca Cloud Alpaca: 131 yds. (120m) per 1¾ oz. (50g) ball
Debbie Bliss Baby Cashmerino: 137 yds. (125m) per 1¾ oz. (50g) ball

Debbie Bliss Cashmerino Astrakhan: 76 yds. (70m) per 1¾ oz. (50g) ball

Debbie Bliss Cashmerino Chunky: 71 yds. (65m) per 1¾ oz. (50g) ball

Debbie Bliss Cathay: 109 yds. (100m) per 1¾ oz. (50g) ball

Jaeger Trinity DK: 218 yds. (200m) per 1¾ oz. (50g) ball

Rowan Big Wool: 87 yds. (70m) per 3½ oz. (100g) ball

Rowan Cashcotton DK: 142 yds. (130m) per 1¾ oz. (50g) ball

Rowan Cashsoft DK: 142 yds. (130m) per 1¾ oz. (50g) ball

Rowan Kid Classic: 153 yds. (140m) per 1¾ oz. (50g) ball

Rowan Kidsilk Haze: 229 yds. (210m) per 1 oz. (25g) ball

Rowan Kidsilk Night: 227 yds. (208m) per 1 oz. (25g) ball

Rowan Wool Cotton DK: 123 yds. (113m) per 1¾ oz. (50g) ball

Sirdar Bigga: 44 yds. (40m) per 3½ oz. (100g) ball

Sirdar Duet: 142 yds. (130m) per 1¾ oz. (50g) ball

Sirdar Foxy: 44 yds. (40m) per 1¾ oz. (50g) ball

Sirdar Wow 63 yds. (58m) per 3½ oz. (100g) ball

Sirdar Yoyo: 962 yds. (880m) per 14 oz. (400g) ball

GAUGE

Always knit a swatch in pattern to obtain the correct gauge. Sweaters have to fit and therefore the single most important thing to achieve that is to get an accurate stitch and row. Without this the garment could end up any shape or size. Knit a swatch which is either a full repeat of the pattern or, if it's a small repeat, a 6 in. (15cm) square. When finished, iron the square under a damp cloth and mark out an area which is 4 in. (10cm) square with pins. If your square turns out to have too many stitches/rows to 4 in. (10cm), then try again using bigger needles; if there are too few stitches, then use smaller needles. Time is precious, so don't waste it by skimping on

swatching. No one wants to spend time knitting a garment they can't wear, so always knit a swatch and remove the uncertainty and stress from your knitting.

STITCHES

The stitches used in the patterns are all straightforward combinations of knit and purl stitches. It is amazing how many different types of knitted fabric can be produced, from smooth stockinette stitch, to stretchy garter stitch, to stitches that are more suited to cuffs, necks, and edges. The following stitches are used throughout the patterns in this book. Any additional stitch combinations are included where relevant at the beginning of each pattern.

1 x 1 rib (odd no sts)
RS rows: *K1, p1, rep from * to last st, k1.
WS rows: *P1, k1, rep from * to last st, p1.

1 x 1 rib (in the round)
Every round: *K1, p1; rep from * around.

2 x 2 rib (multiple of 4 + 2)
RS rows: *K2, p2, rep from * to last 2 sts, k2.
WS rows: *P2, k2, rep from * to last 2 sts, p2.

2 x 2 rib (in the round) *opposite top left*
Every round: *K2, p2; rep from * around.

Stockinette stitch *opposite top right*
RS rows: Knit.
WS rows: Purl.

Stockinette st (in the round)
Knit every round.

Garter stitch *opposite bottom left*
Knit every row.

Garter stitch (in the round)
Row 1: Purl.
Row 2: Knit.

Seed stitch *opposite bottom right*
Row 1: *K1, p1, rep from * to end.
Row 2: K the purl sts and p the knit sts.
Rep Row 2 to end.

FOLLOWING A PATTERN

Always read through the pattern carefully before you start. In the instructions, numbers are given for the smallest size first; larger sizes follow in brackets. When there is only one number, this relates to all sizes. When there are repeat sequences of stitches, this is expressed either through asterisks* or brackets (). For example, a simple 2 x 2 rib would be written *k2, *p2, k2; rep from * to end*, meaning that after the first 2 stitches have been knitted, *p2, k2* would be repeated across the row. Brackets are usually used when a sequence has to be repeated a specific number of times—for example, *k2, (p2, k2) twelve times*, means that after the first 2 stitches have been knitted, *p2, k2* is repeated across the row 12 times in all.

When the pattern calls for a special stitch, this is included at the beginning of each pattern, along with the number of stitches in each repeat of the stitch pattern. For instance, in *Angela* the lace stitch is a multiple of 4+1:

Row 1: K1, *yo, k3, yo, k1; rep from * to end.
Row 2: Purl.
Row 3: K1, *k1, slip 1, k2tog, psso, k2: rep from * to end.
Row 4: Purl.

This means that to center the pattern, you must cast on a multiple of 4 stitches plus one extra, so the least number of stitches you could cast on is 5, but as long as your stitches are divisible by 4 remainder one, then the stitch pattern will always work.

ABBREVIATIONS

alt	alternate	RS	right side
beg	beginning	sl	slip
ch	chain(s)	slip 2-k1-p2sso	slip 2 sts purlwise, k1, then pass 2 slipped sts over at a time, to RH needle. Insert tip of LH needle into fronts of these sts from left to right and knit together
cont	continue		
dc	double crochet		
dec	decrease		
foll	following/follows	ssk	slip 2 sts knitwise, one at a time, then insert LH needle into fronts of these 2 sts and knit together
g st	garter stitch		
inc	increase(e)(ing)		
k	knit	st st	stockinette stitch
k2tog	knit 2 sts together	st(s)	stitch(es)
p	purl	tbl	through back loop
p2tog	purl 2 sts together	tr	treble crochet
patt	pattern	WS	wrong side
psso	pass slipped st over	yb	yarn to back of work
rem	remaining	yf	yarn to front of work
rep	repeat	yo	yarn over needle to make 1 st

FINISHING

Never underestimate the power of blocking and ironing. Small mistakes often become invisible when the overall impression of a piece is spruce and well-presented.

First, neaten selvedges (the sides of a piece of knitting) by sewing/weaving in all the ends along sides or along color joins where appropriate. Then, using pins, block out each piece of knitting to shape. Next, gently iron each piece, omitting ribs, using a warm iron over a damp cloth. Take special care with the edges, because this will make sewing up easier. Keep areas of pattern and texture in line across the sweater, matching the notches made by the selvedge stitches. Take time to pin the garment first and, before sewing, make sure you're satisfied with the way the pieces are fitting together. Unless stated otherwise in the pattern, use a small neat backstitch on the edge of the work for all seams except the ribs, where an invisible edge-to-edge stitch should be used. This method is suitable for all but bulky yarn, for which the mattress stitch can be used. (See page 40.)

CARE OF YARNS AND GARMENTS

Usually handknits should be hand-washed or dry cleaned, although certain fibers can be machine-washed. Always follow the care instructions on the ball band. If hand-washing, use warm water and a mild detergent. Rinse several times until the water runs clear in case the dye runs. Reshape the piece on top of a towel, and then roll it in the towel to remove excess moisture, or spin in the wool cycle of your washing machine. Dry away from direct heat. Always store your knits folded flat and never hung on hangers where they can stretch and lose their shape.

The Collection

Angela

Daytime chic or evening glamour, you can rely on this lacy knit to take you stylishly through the day. This is a great starter project for aspiring lace knitters.

 **Intermediate**

SIZES

	XS	S	M	L	XL	
To fit bust	32	34	36	38	40	in.
	81	86	91	97	102	cm

See diagram on page 19 for actual measurements.

YARN
7 (8:9:10:11) × 1¾ oz. (50g) balls of Rowan Wool Cotton in Aloof 958

NEEDLES
Pair each of US 3 (3.25mm) and US 6 (4mm) needles
4 double pointed US 4 (3.5mm) needles
Stitch holders

GAUGE
19 sts and 28 rows to 10cm (4 in.) measured over lace pattern using US 6 (4mm) needles. Change needle size if necessary to obtain this gauge.

ABBREVIATIONS
See page 12.

STITCHES
1 × 1 rib
Lace pattern (Multiple of 4 + 1)
  Row 1: K1, *yo, k3, yo, k1; rep from * to end.
  Row 2: Purl
  Row 3: K1, *k1, slip 1, k2tog, psso, k2; rep from * to end.
  Row 4: Purl.
  Repeat these 4 rows.

Back

Using smaller needles, cast on 77 (81:89:93:97) sts and work in 1 × 1 rib until work measures 5½ (5½:5½:6:6) in. [14 (14:14:15.25:15.25)cm]. Change to larger needles and refer to lace pattern, repeating the 4 rows to end. Cont until work measures 29.25cm (11½ in.) from cast-on edge, ending on a WS row.

SHAPE ARMHOLE
Bind off 4 (4:4:5:5) sts at beg of next 2 rows. Then dec 1 st at both ends of next and every foll alt row 4 (5:8:8:9) times, keeping pattern correct as set. 61 (63:65:67:69) sts. Cont until work measures 18½ (18½:19:19:19½) in. (47 (47:48.25:48.25:49.5) cm) from cast-on edge, ending on a WS row.

SHAPE NECK AND SHOULDER
Next row: Work 19 (19:20:20:21) sts, place center 23 (25:25:27:27) sts on holder, join a second ball of yarn, and work to end. Working both sides at the same time, dec 1 st at both neck edges on next and foll alt row.
At the same time work and place 5 (5:6:6:6) sts on holder at armhole edge on next row (for left back neck it will be on foll row), and 6 sts on foll alt row. Bind off over all 17 (17:18:18:19) sts.

Front

Work as for Back until work measures
16½ (16½:17:17:17½) in. [42 (42:43:43:44.5)cm]
from cast-on edge ending on a WS row.

SHAPE NECK

Next row: Work 23 (23:24:24:25) sts, place center
15 (17:17:19:19) sts on holder, join a second ball
of yarn and work to end. Working both sides at the
same time, dec 1 st at both neck edges on next and
every foll alt row 6 times. Cont in patt as set until
work measures 18½ (18½:19:19:19½) in.
[47 (47:48.25:48.25:49.5)cm] from cast-on edge,
ending on a WS row.

SHAPE SHOULDERS

Work and place 5 (5:6:6:6) sts on holder at
armhole edge on next row (for left back neck it will
be foll row), then work and place 6 sts on holder
on foll alt row.
Bind off all 17 (17:18:18:19) sts.

Sleeves

Using smaller needles, cast on 45 (45:45:49:49) sts
and work in 1 × 1 rib until work measures
4¼ in. (10.75cm). Change to larger needles and
refer to lace pattern, repeating the 4 rows to end.
At the same time inc as follows:

XS 1 st at both ends of every 21st row 4 times.
53 sts.

S 1 st at both ends of every 17th row 5 times.
55 sts.

M 1 st at both ends of every 13th row 7 times.
59 sts.

L 1 st at both ends of every 11th row 8 times.
65 sts.

XL 1 st at both ends of every 10th row 9 times.
67 sts.

Keep the lace pattern correct adding more repeats
to set pattern on each side as you increase. Cont
until work measures 18 (18:18½:18½:18½) in.
[45.75 (45.75:47:47:47)cm] from cast-on edge,
ending on a WS row.

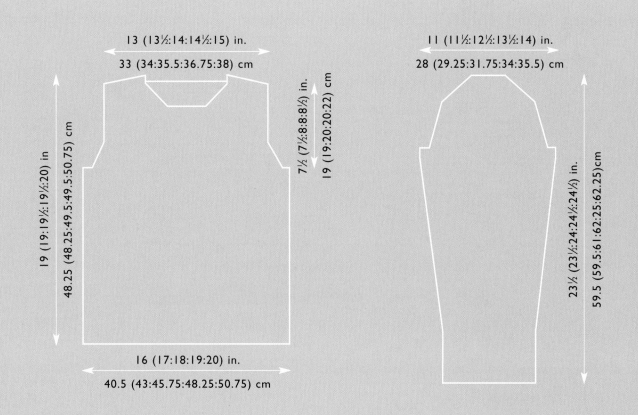

13 (13½:14:14½:15) in.
33 (34:35.5:36.75:38) cm

11 (11½:12½:13½:14) in.
28 (29.25:31.75:34:35.5) cm

7½ (7½:8:8:8½) in.
19 (19:20:20:22) cm

19 (19:19½:19½:20) in
48.25 (48.25:49.5:49.5:50.75) cm

23½ (23½:24:24½:24½) in.
59.5 (59.5:61:62:25:62.25)cm

16 (17:18:19:20) in.
40.5 (43:45.75:48.25:50.75) cm

BACKWARDS LOOP CAST-ON

This is a simple cast-on, useful for casting on stitches in the middle or at the end of a row. It's sometimes used for making a stitch between stitches.

Repeat until you have as many stitches as required.

Make a backwards loop and place it on the needle.

SHAPE SLEEVE CAP

Bind off 4 (4:4:5:5) sts at beg of next 2 rows. Then dec as follows:

XS 1 st at both ends of every 3rd row 8 times, then every alt row 4 times. 21 sts.

S 1 st at both ends of every 3rd row 6 times, then every alt row 7 times. 21 sts.

M 1 st at both ends of every 3rd row twice, then every alt row 13 times. 21 sts.

L 1 st at both ends of every 3rd row 4 times, then every alt row 12 times. 23 sts.

XL 1 st at both ends of every 3rd row twice, then every alt row 15 times. 23 sts.

Bind off 2 sts at beg of next 4 rows.
Bind off rem 13 (13:13:15:15) sts.

Finishing

Join shoulder seams.

NECKBAND

With RS facing and using four US 4 (3.5mm) double pointed needles, starting at point 5 (6:6:7:7) sts in along sts on hold at center front, pick up and knit last 10 (11:11:12:12) sts from holder at center front, 19 sts up front neck edge, 3 sts down right back neck edge, 23 (25:25:27:27) sts from holder at center back, 3 sts up left back neck edge, 19 sts down left front neck, and rem 5 (6:6:7:7) sts from holder at center front, then cast on an extra 5 sts using backward loop cast-on (see above). 87 (91:91:95:95) sts. Then working back and forth, work 1 row as follows:
*P1, k1; rep from * to last st, p1.
Then cont in 1 × 1 rib (working back and forth) for 17 rows, leaving 1 st on st holder (unworked) at both ends of Rows 1, 3, 5, 7, 8, 9, 10, 11 and 12 and leave 2 sts on holder at both ends of Rows 13, 14, 15 and leave 3 sts on holder at both ends of Rows 16 and 17, keeping patt correct as set. Then starting at RS front edge, place all sts on needle again (87 (91:91:95:95) sts) and bind off in rib over all sts, picking up and knitting 1 st as you bind off between sts 0 and 1, 1 and 2, 2 and 3, 3 and 4, at both sides, so that there are no holes. Stitch bottom edge (extra stitches) of collar neatly in place horizontally along inside center front. Set in sleeves, easing any fullness evenly across top of cap. Sew side and sleeve seams in one line.

Kelly

Bold, graphic stripes make a confident statement in this longline sweater. For a restrained sophisticated look, try striping with two similar hues, or two tones of one color.

 Beginner

SIZES

	XS	S	M	L	XL	
To fit bust	32	34	36	38	40	in.
	81	86	91	97	102	cm

See diagram on page 24 for actual measurements.

YARN

7 (7:8:9:10) x 1¾ oz. (50g) balls of Sirdar Duet in White 747 (A)
3 (3:4:5:5) x 1¾ oz. (50g) balls of Sirdar Duet in Black 745 (B)

NEEDLES

Pair each of US 6 (4mm) and US 8 (5mm) needles
Stitch holders

GAUGE

21 sts and 28 rows to 4 in. (10cm) measured over pattern using US 8 (5mm) needles. Change needle size if necessary to obtain this gauge.

ABBREVIATIONS

See page 12.

STITCHES

1 x 1 rib
Stockinette stitch
Striped pattern
   Stripe 1: Work 3¼ in. (8.25cm) in A (including rib).
   Stripe 2: Work 1½ in. (3.8cm) in B.
   Stripe 3: Work 2¾ (2¾:2¾:3:3) in. [7 (7:7:7.5:7.5)cm] in A.
   Stripe 4: Work 1½ in. (3.8cm) in B.
   Repeat Stripes 3 and 4 three more times (10 stripes)
   Stripe 11 (Front): Work 2¾ in. (7cm) in A – 24½ (24½:24½:25½:25½) in. [62.25 (62.25:62.25:64.75:64.75)cm] including rib.
   Stripe 11 (Back): Work 4¼ in. (10.8cm) in A – 26 (26:26:27:27) in. [66 (66:66:68.5:68.5)cm] including rib.

Back

Using smaller needles and A, cast on 89 (95:99:105:111) sts and work 1¼ in. (3cm) in k1, p1 rib, ending on a WS row. Change to larger needles and cont in st st in striped pattern. Cont until work measures 19½ (19¼:19:19¾:19½) in. [49.5 (48.75:48.25:50:49.5)cm] from cast-on edge, ending on a WS row.

SHAPE ARMHOLE

Dec 1 st at both ends of next and every foll alt row 8 (10:10:12:14) times in all, keeping striped patt correct. 73 (75:79:81:83) sts.
Cont as set until work measures 25 (25:25:26:26) in. [63.5 (63.5:63.5:66:66)cm], ending on a WS row and then change to smaller needles and work 1 in. (2.5cm) in k1, p1, rib ending on a WS row, keeping striped pattern correct.

Next row (RS): Cont to end in rib and A, work 13 sts, place center 47 (49:53:55:57) sts on holder, join a second ball of yarn and work to end. Working both sides at the same time, place 1 st on holder at both neck edges on next and foll alt row 13 times, keeping rib correct.

Front

Work as for Back until work measures 23½ (23½:23½:24½:24½) in. [59.5 (59.5:59.5:62.25:62.25)cm], ending on a WS row and then change to smaller needles and work 1 in. (2.5cm) in k1, p1, rib, keeping striped pattern correct. Bind off loosely in rib.

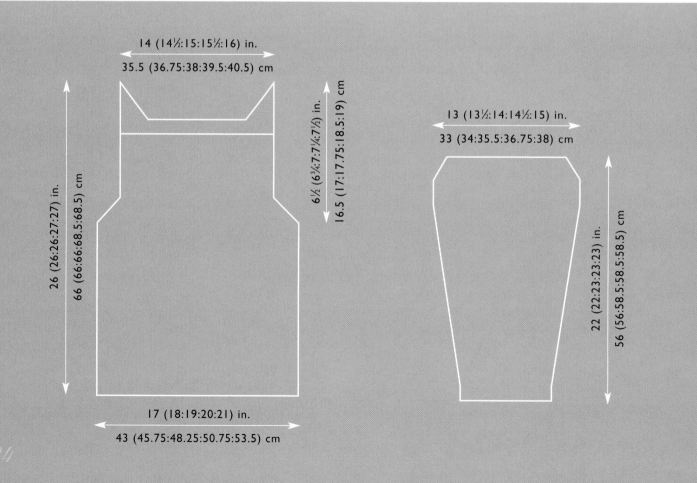

14 (14½:15:15½:16) in.
35.5 (36.75:38:39.5:40.5) cm

6½ (6¾:7:7¼:7½) in.
16.5 (17:17.75:18.5:19) cm

26 (26:26:27:27) in.
66 (66:66:68.5:68.5) cm

17 (18:19:20:21) in.
43 (45.75:48.25:50.75:53.5) cm

13 (13½:14:14½:15) in.
33 (34:35.5:36.75:38) cm

22 (22:23:23:23) in.
56 (56:58.5:58.5:58.5) cm

Sleeves

Using smaller needles and A, cast on
47 (47:47:49:49) sts and work 1¼ in. (3cm) in k1,
p1 rib, ending on WS row. Change to larger
needles and cont in st st in striped pattern,
adjusting the first stripe so that stripes match at
armholes as follows:

Stripe 1: Work 3½ (3½:4¼:3:3½) in.
[8.9 (8.9:10.8:7.6:8.9)cm] in A (including rib).
Work other stripes as set.
At the same time inc after rib as follows:

XS 1 st at both ends of every 10th row 3 times,
then every 11th row 8 times. 69 sts.

S 1 st at both ends of every 9th row 4 times,
then every 10th row 8 times. 71 sts.

M 1 st at both ends of every 9th row 10 times,
then every 10th row 3 times. 73 sts.

L 1 st at both ends of every 8th row 10 times,
then every 9th row 4 times. 77 sts.

XL 1 st at both ends of every 7th row 6 times,
then every 8th row 9 times. 79 sts.

Cont as set until work measures 19¾
(19½:20:19½:19¼) in. [50 (49.5:50.75:49.5:49)cm].

TOP OF SLEEVE

Dec 1 st at both ends of next and every foll alt row
8 (10:10:12:14) times in all, keeping striped patt
correct. Bind off rem 53 (51:53:53:51) sts loosely.

Finishing

BACK NECK EDGE

Using smaller needles and A, with RS facing and
starting at right armhole edge, pick up and rib
(starting with p1) 25 sts down sloping edge (1 from
every holder and 1 extra st between each of the sts
on hold), rib 47 (49:53:55:57) sts from holder at
center back and rib 25 sts up other sloping edge as
before. 97 (99:103:105:107) sts. Bind off in rib.
Place the wings on back to overlap fronts by 2 in.
(5cm), (1½ in. (3.75cm) will be front neck drop)
and stitch in place along armhole edge.
Set in sleeves placing any fullness evenly over
whole sleeve cap. Join side and sleeve seams in
one line.

Gabrielle

This flirty, easy-to-knit sweater in funky yarn changes color as you knit. Whether you're dressed to kill or relaxing in jeans, you can count on this sweater to add the feel-good factor.

 **Beginner**

SIZES

	XS	S	M	L	XL	
To fit bust	32	34	36	38	40	in.
	81	86	91	97	102	cm

See diagram on page 29 for actual measurements.

YARN

1 x 14 oz. (400g) ball of Sirdar Yoyo in Purple Haze 013 (A)
1 x 1¾ oz. (50g) ball of Sirdar Foxy in Silver Fox 434 (B)

NEEDLES

Pair each of US 5 (3.75mm), US 7 (4.5mm) and US 9 (5.5mm) needles
US 9 (5.5mm) circular needle
Stitch holders

GAUGE

15 sts and 24 rows to 4 in. (10cm) measured over stockinette stitch using US 7 (4.5mm) needles.

ABBREVIATIONS

See page 12.

STITCHES

Garter stitch
Stockinette stitch

Back

Take yarn from center of the ball.
Using US 5 (3.75mm) needles and A cast on 60 (64:68:72:76) sts. Knit 4 rows and then change to US 7 (4.5mm) needles and cont in st st to end, dec as follows:

XS 1 st at both ends of every 5th row 4 times. 52 sts.

S 1 st at both ends of every 6th row once, then every 7th row twice. 58 sts.

M 1 st at both ends of every 7th row twice, then every 8th row once. 62 sts.

L 1 st at both ends of every 7th row twice, then every 8th row once. 66 sts.

XL 1 st at both ends of every 8th row once, then every 9th row twice. 70 sts.

Work a further 8 rows, then inc 1 st at both ends of next and every foll 8th (12th:12th:10th:10th) row 4 (3:3:3:3) times in all. 60 (64:68:72:76) sts.
Cont as set until work measures 11½ (11½:11½: 11:11½) in. [29.25 (29.25:29.25:28:29.25)cm] from cast-on edge, ending on a WS row.

SHAPE ARMHOLE

Bind off 3 (3:4:4:4) sts at beg of next 2 rows, then dec 1 st at both ends of next and every alt row 3 (3:4:5:6) times. 48 (52:52:54:56) sts.
Cont as set until work measures 18½ (18½:19: 19:19½) in. [47 (47:48.25:48.25:49.5)cm] from cast-on edge, ending on a WS row.

SHAPE SHOULDER AND NECK

Next row (RS): Work 14 (16:15:16:17) sts, place center 20 (20:22:22:22) sts on holder, join a second ball of yarn (leave enough yarn to finish right back neck edge and rejoin at left neck edge) and work to end. Working both sides at the same time, dec 1 st at both neck edges on next and foll alt row.

At the same time work and place 4 (4:4:4:5) sts on holder at armhole edge on next row, (for left back neck it will be foll row), and 4 (5:4:5:5) sts on foll alt row. Bind off over whole 12 (14:13:14:15) sts.

Front

Take yarn from outside of the ball.
Work as for Back until work measures 14 (14:14½:14½:15) in. [35.5 (35.5: 36.75:36.75:38)cm], ending on a WS row.

SHAPE NECKLINE

Next row (RS): Work 12 (14:13:14:15) sts, place center 24 (24:26:26:26) sts on holder, join a second ball of yarn (leave enough yarn to finish left front neck edge and rejoin at right neck edge) and work to end. Working both sides at the same time, cont until work measures 18½ (18½:19:19:19½) in. [47 (47:48.25:48.25:49.5)cm] from cast-on edge, ending on a WS row (RS row for right neck edge).

SHAPE SHOULDER

Work and place 4 (4:4:4:5) sts on holder at armhole edge, work to end of row. Work 1 row. Work and place 4 (5:4:5:5) sts on holder at armhole edge, work to end of row. Work 1 row. Bind off over all 12 (14:13:14:15) sts.

Sleeves

For 1st sleeve take yarn from center of the ball. For 2nd sleeve take yarn from outside of the ball. Using US 9 (5.5mm) needles and B, cast on 30 (30:30:32:32) sts. Knit 6 rows and then change to US 7 (4.5mm) needles and A and cont in st st to end, inc as follows:

XS 1 st at both ends of every 15th row 6 times. 42 sts.

S 1 st at both ends of every 13th row 7 times. 44 sts.

M 1 st at both ends of every 12th row 8 times. 46 sts.

L 1 st at both ends of every 10th row 3 times, then every 11th row 6 times. 50 sts.

XL 1 st at both ends of every 9th row 4 times, then every 10th row 6 times. 52 sts.

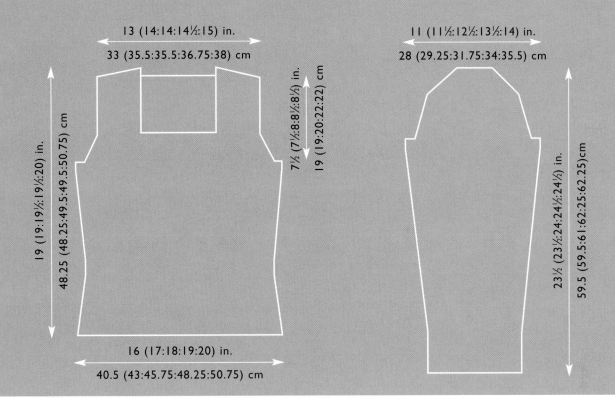

Diagram labels:

13 (14:14:14½:15) in.
33 (35.5:35.5:36.75:38) cm

7½ (7½:8:8½:8½) in.
19 (19:20:22:22) cm

19 (19:19½:19½:20) in.
48.25 (48.25:49.5:49.5:50.75) cm

16 (17:18:19:20) in.
40.5 (43:45.75:48.25:50.75) cm

11 (11½:12½:13½:14) in.
28 (29.25:31.75:34:35.5) cm

23½ (23½:24:24½:24½) in.
59.5 (59.5:61:62:62.25) cm

Cont in patt as set until work measures 18 (18:18½:18½:18½) in. [45.75 (45.75:47:47:47)cm] from cast-on edge, ending on a WS row.

SHAPE SLEEVE CAP

Bind off 3 (3:4:4:4) sts at beg of next 2 rows, then dec 1 st at both ends of next row and then dec as follows:

XS 1 st at both ends of every foll 4th row 3 times, then every 3rd row 5 times. 18 sts.

S 1 st at both ends of every foll 3rd row 9 times. 18 sts.

M 1 st at both ends of every foll 4th row 3 times, then every 3rd row 5 times. 20 sts.

L 1 st at both ends of every foll 3rd row 10 times. 20 sts.

XL 1 st at both ends of every foll 3rd row 8 times, then every alt row 3 times. 20 sts.

Bind off 2 sts at beg of next 4 rows. Bind off rem 10 (10:12:12:12) sts.

Finishing

Set in sleeves.
Sew side and sleeve seams in one line.

NECKBAND

With RS facing and using US 9 (5.5mm) circular needle and B, starting at left shoulder seam, pick up and k19 sts down front neck edge, k24 (24:26:26:26) sts from holder at center front, k19 sts up left side neck edge, 2 sts down left back neck edge, 20 (20:22:22:22) sts from holder at center back and 2 sts up right back neck edge. 86 (86:90:90:90) sts. Join into the round and work 6 rows in garter st (see page 10) as follows:

Round 1: Purl.

Round 2: Knit, dec 1 st at both corner edges at center front.

Rounds 3–6: Rep rounds 1 and 2 respectively. Bind off purlwise over 80 (80:84:84:84) sts.

Rebecca

A modern take on the classic fifties bolero. The sleeves are integrated into the back and fronts making for easier finishing with no sleeves to set in.

★ ☆ ☆ Beginner

SIZES

	XS	S	M	L	XL	
To fit bust	32	34	36	38	40	in.
	81	86	91	97	102	cm

See diagram on page 33 for actual measurements.

YARN

5 (5:6:6:6) × 1¾ oz. (50g) balls of Rowan Cashcotton DK in Pool 602

NEEDLES

Pair of US 6 (4mm) needles

NOTIONS

1 large button

GAUGE

22 sts and 28 rows to 4 in. (10cm) measured over stockinette stitch. Change needle size if necessary to obtain this gauge.

ABBREVIATIONS

See page 12.

STITCHES

Stockinette stitch
Seed stitch

Back

Cast on 68 (74:80:86:92) sts.
Row 1: Slip 1, knit to end of row.
Row 2: Slip 1, purl to last st, k1.
Cont in st st, inc once at each end of the next and every foll 6th row until there are 80 (86:92:98:104) sts.
Next row: Slip 1, purl to last st, k1.
Cont in st st, inc once at each end of the next and every alt row until there are 98 (104:110:116:122) sts.
Next row: Slip 1, purl to last st, k1.
Cont in st st, inc 1 st at each end of every row until there are 118 (124:130:136:142) sts.
Next row: Slip 1, knit to end of row, cast on 12 sts.
Next row: K1, purl to end of row, cast on 12 sts. 142 (148:154:160:166) sts.
Work 40 rows in st st without shaping.

SHAPE SHOULDERS

Bind off 9 sts at beg of each of the next 8 rows.
Bind off 8 (9:10:11:12) sts at beg of each of the next 6 rows.
Bind off the rem 22 sts.

Left Front

Cast on 2 sts.
Row 1: Slip 1, k1, cast on 2 sts.
Row 2 and every alt row: K1, purl to last st, k1.

Row 3: Slip 1, inc once in the next st, k2, cast on 2 (2:2:3:3) sts.

Rows 5 and 7: Slip 1, knit to end of row, cast on 2 (2:2:3. 3) sts.

Row 9: Slip 1, inc once in the next st, knit to end of row, cast on 2 (2:3:3:3) sts.

Rows 11 and 13: Slip 1, knit to end of row, cast on 2 (2:3:3:3) sts.

Row 15: Slip 1, inc once in the next st, knit to end of row, cast on 3 (3:3:3:4) sts.

Rows 17 and 19: Slip 1, knit to end of row, cast on 2 (3:3:3:3) sts.

Row 21: As Row 15.

Row 23: Slip 1, knit to end of row, cast on 2 (3:3:3:3) sts.

Row 25: Slip 1, knit to end of row, cast on 3 (3:3:3:4) sts.

Row 26: K1, purl to last st, k1. 35 (38:41:44:47) sts.

Next row: Slip 1, inc once in the next st, knit to last 2 sts, k2tog.

Beg with a purl row, work 5 rows in st st without shaping.

Next row: Slip 1, inc once in next st, knit to end of row.

Next row: Slip 1, purl to last st, k1.

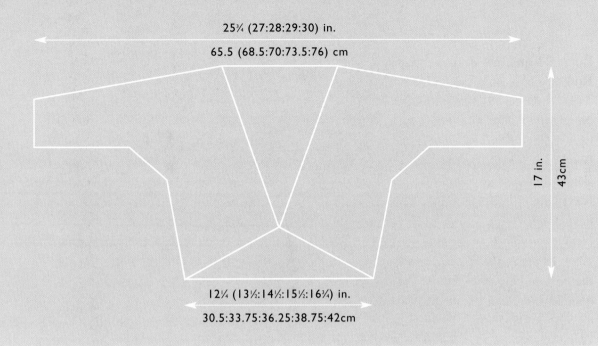

25¾ (27:28:29:30) in.

65.5 (68.5:70:73.5:76) cm

17 in.

43cm

12¼ (13½:14½:15½:16¾) in.

30.5:33.75:36.25:38.75:42cm

Work 18 rows in st st, inc once at the beg of next and every alt row, *at the same time* dec once at the front edge (as before) in the next and every foll 8th row. 42 (45:48:51:54) sts.

Work 10 rows in st st, inc once at the side edge in every row, *at the same time* dec once at the front edge (as before) in the 7th row. 51 (54:57:60:63) sts.

Next row: Slip 1, knit to end of row.

Next row: Slip 1, purl to end of row, cast on 12 sts.

Work 19 rows in st st, dec once at the front edge (as before) in the 3rd and every following 8th row. 60 (63:66:69:72) sts.

Beg with a purl row work 21 rows in st st without shaping.

SHAPE SHOULDER

Row 1: Bind off 9 sts, knit to end of row.

Row 2: Slip 1, purl to end of row.

Repeat these 2 rows 3 times.

Row 9: Bind off 8 (9:10:11:12) sts, knit to end of row.

Row 10: Slip 1, purl to end of row.

Repeat the Rows 9 and 10 once. Bind off remaining 8 (9:10:11:12) sts.

Right Front

Cast on 2 sts.

Row 1: Slip 1, k1.

Row 2: Slip 1, p1, cast on 2 sts.

Row 3: K1, inc once in the next st, k2.

Rows 4, 6 and 8: Slip 1, purl to end of row, cast on 2 (2:2:3:3) sts.

Rows 5 and 7: Knit to end of row.

Row 9: Knit to the last 3 sts, inc once in the next st, k2.

Rows 10 and 12: Slip 1, purl to end of row, cast on 2 (2:3:3:3) sts.

Row 14: Slip 1, purl to end of row, cast on 2 (2:3:3:4) sts.

Rows 11 and 13: Knit to end of row.

Row 15: As Row 9.

Rows 16 and 18: Slip 1, purl to end of row, cast on 2 (3:3:3:3) sts.

Rows 17 and 19: Knit to end of row.

Row 20: Slip 1, purl to end of row, cast on 2 (3:3:3:4) sts.

Row 21: As Row 9.

Rows 22 and 24: Slip 1, purl to end of row, cast on 3 sts.

Nicole

A *chunky fitted jacket which knits up in a flash. This is a great project for a relaxed weekend with your knitting, it's guaranteed to banish the Monday-morning blues.*

 Beginner

SIZES

	XS	S	M	L	XL	
To fit bust	32	34	36	38	40	in.
	81	86	91	97	102	cm

See diagram on page 38 for actual measurements.

YARN
5 (6:6:7:7) × 3½ oz. (100g) balls of Rowan Big Wool in Wild Berry 025

NEEDLES
Pair each of US 13 (9mm), US 15 (10mm) and US 17 (12mm) needles
Stitch holders

NOTIONS
3 large buttons

GAUGE
8 sts and 10 rows to 4 in. (10cm) measured over stockinette stitch using US 17 (12mm) needles. Change needle size if necessary to obtain this gauge.

ABBREVIATIONS
See page 12.

STITCHES
Seed stitch
Stockinette stitch

Back

Using medium-size needles cast on 33 (35:37:39:41) sts and work 1½ in. (3.75cm) in seed st, ending on a WS row. Change to larger needles and work to end in st st, dec 1 st at both ends of next and foll 8th (8th:8th:10th:10th) row twice. 29 (31:33:35:37) sts. Work 5 rows without shaping, then inc 1 st at both ends of next and foll 8th row twice. 33 (35:37:39:41) sts. Cont until work measures 12½ (12½:13:13:13) in. [31.75 (31.75:33:33:33)cm] from cast-on edge, ending on a WS row.

SHAPE ARMHOLE
Bind off 2 sts at beg of next 2 rows. Then dec 1 st at both ends of next, then every row 0 (0:0:0:2) times, then every alt row 1 (4:4:5:4) times, then every 3rd row 2 (0:0:0:0) times.

WORK NECKLINE
At the same time starting on row 7 (7:7:9:9) of armhole decreases (excluding bind off rows), work 1 (2:2:2:2) sts as set, k2tog. Join a second ball of yarn, bind off next 17 (17:19:19:19) sts, k2tog, work 1 (2:2:2:2) sts as set. Working both sides at the same time, work rem armhole decs simultaneously. Bind off last st.

Left Front

Using medium-size needles cast on
21 (22:23:24:25) sts and work 1½ in. (3.75cm) in
seed st, ending on WS row. Change to larger
needles and work to end in st st, dec 1 st at beg of
next and foll 8th (8th:8th:10th:10th) row twice.
19 (20:21:22:23) sts. Work 5 rows without shaping,
then inc 1 st at beg of next and foll 8th row twice.
21 (22:23:24:25) sts. Cont until work measures
12½ (12½:13:13:13) in. [31.75 (31.75:33:33:33)cm]
from cast-on edge, ending on a WS row.

SHAPE ARMHOLE

Bind off 2 sts at beg of next row. Work 1 row.
Then dec 1 st at armhole edge of next, then
every row 0 (0:0:0:2) times, then every alt row
1 (4:4:5:4) times, then every 3rd row
2 (0:0:0:0) times. 15 (15:16:16:18) sts.

WORK NECKLINE

At the same time starting on row 7 (7:7:9:9) of
armhole decreases, work 1 (2:2:2:2) sts as set,
k2tog, bind off next 13 (13:14:14:14) sts.
Work rem armhole decs. Bind off last st.

Right Front

Mark position of 2 buttons on Left Front, first one
5½ (5½:6:6½:6½) in. [14 (14:15.25:16.5:16.5)cm]
up from cast-on edge and second 4 in. (10cm)
down from center front neck edge. Work as for
Left Front reversing all shapings and inserting
buttonholes opposite markers on RS rows to
correspond to markers on Left Front as follows:
Next row: Work 2 sts, bind off 3 sts, work to end
of row.
Next row: Work to last 5 sts, cast on 3 sts,
work 2 sts.
Work in back of 3 cast-on sts on next row.

Sleeves

Using medium-size needles cast on
19 (19:19:21:21) sts and work 4 in. (10cm) in seed
st, ending on a WS row. Change to larger needles

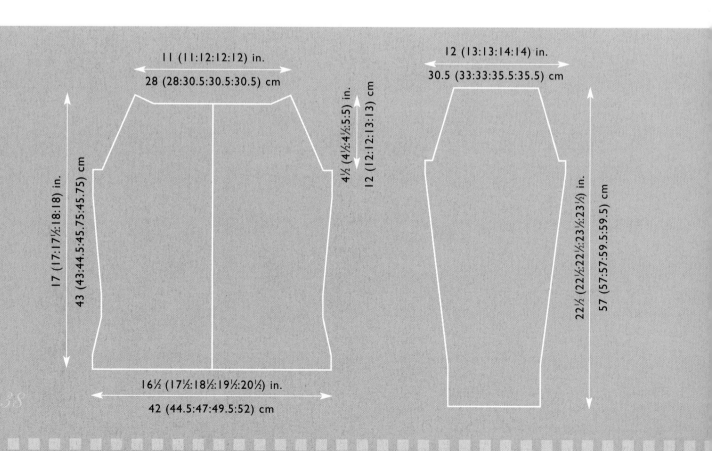

11 (11:12:12:12) in.
28 (28:30.5:30.5:30.5) cm

4½ (4½:4½:5:5) in.
12 (12:12:13:13) cm

17 (17:17½:18:18) in.
43 (43:44.5:45.75:45.75) cm

16½ (17½:18½:19½:20½) in.
42 (44.5:47:49.5:52) cm

12 (13:13:14:14) in.
30.5 (33:33:35.5:35.5) cm

22½ (22½:22½:23½:23½) in.
57 (57:57:59.5:59.5) cm

and work to end in st st, inc 1 st at both ends of every 7th row 0 (2:2:0:0) times, then every 8th row 0 (2:2:4:4) times, then every 10th row 3 (0:0:0:0) times. 25 (27:27:29:29) sts.
Cont until work measures 18 (18:18:18½:18½) in. [45.75 (45.75:45.75:47:47)cm] from cast-on edge.

MATTRESS STITCH

Thread a blunt needle with yarn. Working between the selvedge and the next stitch, pick up 2 bars. Cross to matching place in opposite piece and pick up 2 bars. *Return to first piece, go down into the hole you came out of, and pick up 2 bars. Return to opposite piece, go down into the hole you came out of, and pick up 2 bars. Repeat from * across, pulling the thread taut as you go.

SHAPE SLEEVE CAP
Bind off 2 sts at beg of next 2 rows.
Then dec 1 st at both ends of every 3rd row 0 (0:0:1:1) times, then every alt row 4 times, then every row 1 (1:1:0:0) times. 11 (13:13:15:15) sts. Bind off these sts.

Finishing

Use mattress stitch for all seams (see left). Join raglan seams.
Join side and sleeve seams in one line. Turn back cuffs and stitch in place at end of seam (one place only, not all around).

COLLAR
Using smallest needles, starting at right center front neck edge, with RS facing, pick up and k12 (12:13:13:13) sts from holder, k2 sts up neck edge, 10 (12:12:14:14) sts across top of right sleeve, k2 sts down back neck, k15 (15:17:17:17) sts from holder at center back, k2 sts up back neck edge, 10 (12:12:14:14) sts across top of left sleeve, k2 sts down left front neck edge and k12 (12:13:13:13) sts from holder at left center front neck edge. 67 (71:75:79:79) sts.
Work 4 in. (10cm) in seed st, and then bind off in seed st.
At the same time when 2 in. (5cm) have been worked, ending on WS row, work buttonhole on RS row as before.

RIGHT FRONT BAND
Using US 15 (10mm) needles, with RS facing and starting at bottom edge, pick up and k40 (40:40: 42:42) sts evenly along center front edge and side of collar. Bind off knitwise.

LEFT FRONT BAND
Work as for Right front band, starting at center front neck edge at top of collar.

Eve

I've always loved skirts with a basque for their flattering shape. If you're new to knitting in the round, this is a good project. The skirt has a fun edging technique to add to your repertoire.

 ## Intermediate

SIZES

	XS	S	M	L	XL	
To fit hips	32	34	36	38	40	in.
	81	86	91	97	102	cm

See diagram on page 43 for actual measurements.

YARN

6 (6:7:7:8) × 1¾ oz. (50g) balls of Rowan Kid Classic in Crystal 840

NOTIONS

1⅔ yd (1.5 m) × 1 in. (2.5cm) ribbon

NEEDLES

Pair of US 7 (4.5mm) needles
US 6 (4mm), US 7 (4.5mm) and US 9 (5.5mm) circular needles

GAUGE

18 sts and 24 rows to 4 in. (10cm) measured over stockinette stitch using US 9 (5.5mm) needles. Change needle size if necessary to obtain this gauge.

ABBREVIATIONS

See page 12.

STITCHES

Stockinette stitch (back and forth)
Stockinette stitch (in the round)
2 x 2 rib (in the round)

Skirt (worked in one piece)

Using straight needles cast on 204 (216:222:234: 246) sts and starting with a knit row, working back and forth, work 8 rows in st st.

Next row (RS): K6, then rotate the LH needle counterclockwise through 360 degrees (a whole circle), then k another 6 sts and rotate the LH needle again counter-clockwise through 360 degrees. Cont to k6 sts and rotate LH needle to end of row. Change to US 9 (5.5mm) circular needle, join work into the round, taking care to have the rolled rev st st edge on RS, and work in the round in st st (knit every row on outside) to end. Cont as set until work measures 18 (18:18:18½:18½) in. [45.75 (45.75:45.75:47:47)cm], dec 28 (28:30:30:34) sts evenly across final row. 176 (188:192:204:212) sts.

WORK BASQUE
Change to US 7 (4.5mm) circular needle and work in 2 × 2 rib in the round for 5 (5:5:5½:5½) in. [12.75 (12.75:12.75:14:14)cm]. Change to US 6 (4mm) circular needle and work a further 2 in. (5cm) in 2 × 2 rib.

EYELET ROW
Next row: *K2, yo, p2tog; rep from * around. Work a further 1 in. (2.5cm) in 2 × 2 rib and then bind off in rib.

Finishing

Sew together rolled hem on inside.
Thread ribbon through eyelets and tie in center.

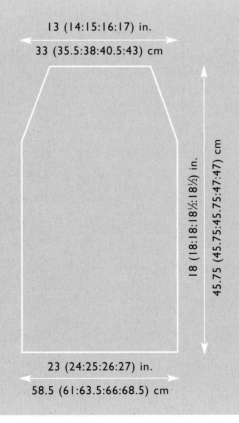

13 (14:15:16:17) in.
33 (35.5:38:40.5:43) cm

18 (18:18:18½:18½) in.
45.75 (45.75:45.75:47:47) cm

23 (24:25:26:27) in.
58.5 (61:63.5:66:68.5) cm

Linda

This pretty summer top looks just as good adding pizzazz underneath a business suit, as when given center stage with cropped pants or jeans.

★ ★ ☆ Intermediate

SIZES

	XS	S	M	L	XL	
To fit bust	32	34	36	38	40	in.
	81	86	91	97	102	cm

See diagram on page 46 for actual measurements.

YARN
6 (6:7:7:8) × 1¾ oz. (50g) balls of Debbie Bliss Cathay in Blue 08 (A)
1 (1:1:2:2) × 1¾ oz. (50g) balls of Debbie Bliss Cathay in White 02 (B)

NEEDLES
Pair each of US 3 (3.25mm) and US 5 (3.75mm) needles
US 3 (3.25mm) circular needle
Stitch holders

GAUGE
22 sts and 30 rows 4 in. (10cm) measured over stockinette stitch using US 5 (3.75mm) needles. Change needle size if necessary to obtain this gauge.

ABBREVIATIONS
See page 12.

STITCHES
Garter stitch
Stockinette stitch

Front and Back (both alike)

Using A and smaller needles, cast on 88 (94:100:104:110) sts and knit 4 rows. Change to larger needles and continue in st st in A to end, dec as follows:
XS and S 1 st at both ends of every 5th row 5 times. 78 (84) sts.
M, L and XL 1 st at both ends of every 7th row twice, then every 8th row twice. 92 (96:102) sts. Work a further 10 rows, then inc as follows:
XS and S 1 st at both ends of every 6th row 5 times. 88 (94) sts.
M and XL 1 st at both ends of every 6th row twice, then every 7th row twice. 100 (110) sts.
L 1 st at both ends of every 5th row twice, then every 6th row twice. 104 sts.
Cont until work measures 11½ in. (29.25cm) from cast-on edge, ending on a WS row.

SHAPE ARMHOLE
Bind off 4 (4:4:5:5) sts at beg of next 2 rows.
Then dec 1 st at both ends of next and every alt row 4 times. Purl 1 row.

SHAPE NECK
Next row (RS): K2tog, k23 (26:29:30:33) sts, bind off 22 sts, k22 (22:25:26:28) sts, k2tog, turn.
Work on last set of k24 (27:30:31:34) sts only.
Next row: Purl.
Next row: Bind off 4 sts, k to last 2 sts, k2tog.
Next row: Purl.

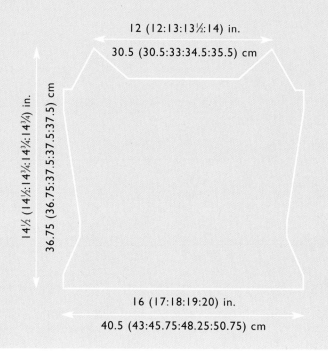

12 (12:13:13½:14) in.
30.5 (30.5:33:34.5:35.5) cm

14½ (14½:14¾:14¾:14¾) in.
36.75 (36.75:37.5:37.5:37.5) cm

16 (17:18:19:20) in.
40.5 (43:45.75:48.25:50.75) cm

11 (11½:12½:12½:13) in.
28 (29.25:31.75:31.75:33) cm

7½ (7½:7¾:7½:7¾) in.
19 (19:19.5:19.5:19.5) cm

Next row: Bind off 3 (4:4:4:4) sts, k to last 2 sts, k2tog.

Next row: Purl.

Next row: Bind off 3 (4:3:4:4) sts, k to last 2 sts, k2tog.

Next row: Purl.

Next row: Bind off 3 (3:3:3:4) sts, k to last 2 sts, k2tog.

Next row: Purl.

Next row: Bind off 3 (3:3:3:4) sts, k to last 2 sts, k2tog.

Next row: Purl.

Next row: Bind off 2 (3:3:3:4) sts, k to last 2 sts, k2tog.

Next row: Purl.

Next row: Bind off 0 (0:3:3:3) sts, k to last 2 sts, k2tog.

Next row: Purl.

Fasten off. Complete other side to match, reversing shapings.

Sleeves

Using B and smaller needles, cast on 60 (62:68:70:72) sts and knit 2 rows. Change to A and knit 2 rows. Work a further 10 rows in BBAA sequence, ending on B. Change to larger needles and continue in st st in A to end. Cont until work measures 4½ in. (11.5cm) from cast-on edge, ending with a WS row.

SHAPE TOP OF SLEEVE

Bind off 4 (4:4:5:5) sts at beg of next 2 rows. Then dec 1 st at both ends of every alt row 10 (10:11:11:11) times, ending on a WS row. Leave rem 32 (34:38:38:40) sts on holder.

Finishing

Join the sleeves to the back and front pieces.

NECKBAND

Using circular needle and B, with RS facing and starting at center front, pick up and k33 (33:35:37:39) sts from center front to armhole, work across 32 (34:38:38:40) sts of one sleeve, then pick up 66 sts round back neck, work across 32 (34:38:38:40) sts of the other sleeve, and then pick up and k33 (33:35:37:39) sts to center front. 196 (200:212:216:224) sts. Cont in garter st in the round as follows:

Next round: Purl using B.
Next round: Knit using A.
Next round: Purl using A.
Next round: Knit using B.
Rep these 4 rounds twice more, then work first round (13 rounds in all) and then bind off knitwise in B.

THE BOW

Using smaller needles and B cast on 68 sts and work in 14 rows in garter st (knit every row) 2 row stripes, ending with B. For the knot, cast on 16 sts and work as for bow. Bind off.

Sew side and sleeve seams in one line. Fold bow piece in half so that ends meet in center and stitch. Fold knot piece over the center of bow strip and stitch at center back. Stitch bow firmly to center front of neckband and secure edges.

Grace

With its crocheted midriff, this fitted cap-sleeved dress gives the perfect mixed message of demure sexiness and is a staple for summer nights on the town.

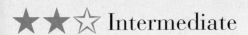 **Intermediate**

SIZES

	XS	S	M	L	XL	
To fit bust	32	34	36	38	40	in.
	81	86	91	97	102	cm
To fit hips	34	36	38	40	42	in.
	86	91	97	102	107	cm

See diagram on page 52 for actual measurements.

YARN

7 (7:8:9:10) × 1¾ oz. (50g) balls of Jaeger Trinity DK in Lipstick 440

NEEDLES

Pair each of US 3 (3.25mm), US 5 (3.75mm) and US 6 (4mm) needles
One each of US D3 (3.25mm), US E4 (3.75mm) and US F5 (4mm) crochet hooks
Stitch markers and holders

GAUGE

22 sts and 30 rows to 4 in. (10cm) measured over stockinette stitch using US 6 (4mm) needles. Change needle size if necessary to obtain this gauge.

ABBREVIATIONS

See page 12.

STITCHES

Stockinette stitch
Single crochet
Double crochet

Skirt (back and front alike)

Using US 3 (3.25mm) needles cast on 103 (109:115:121:127) sts and work in st st for 9 rows, ending with a knit row. Knit next row to mark turning of hem.

Change to US 6 (4mm) needles and, beg with a RS row, cont in st st until work measures 16 (16:17:17:17) in. [40.5 (40.5:43:43:43)cm] from hemline, ending with a WS row.

Next row: K22 (25:28:31:34) sts, k2 tog tbl, k55, k2tog, k22 (25:28:31:34) sts. Work 3 rows without shaping.

Next row: K22 (25:28:31:34) sts, k2 tog tbl, k53, k2tog, k22 (25:28:31:34) sts. Work 3 rows without shaping.

Cont dec in this way, working 2 sts less at center on next and every foll 4th row until 77 (83:89:95:101) sts rem.

Cont without shaping until work measures 23 (23:24:24:24) in. [58.5 (58.5:61:61:61)cm] from hemline, ending with a WS row. Knit 2 rows. Bind off purlwise.

Top (back and front alike)

Using US 6 (4mm) needles cast on 95 (101:107: 113:119) sts and knit 2 rows. Cont in st st until work measures 3 in. (7.5cm), ending with a WS row.

SHAPE ARMHOLES

Bind off 5 (6:7:7:8) sts at beg of next 2 rows.
Dec 1 st both ends of every row until
75 (77:79:81:83) sts rem.
Cont without shaping until armhole measures 6
(6¼:6½:6½:6¾) in. [15.25 (16:16.5:16.5:17)cm]
from beg, measured on straight of work, ending on
a WS row.

SHAPE NECK

Next row: K27 (28:29:30:31) sts, turn, finish this
side first, leave other sts on spare needle.
** Bind off at neck edge on alt rows, 3 sts once,
2 sts, then dec 1 st at neck edge on next 4 alt rows.
At the same time when armhole measures
7 (7¼:7½:7½:7¾) in. [17.75 (18.5:19:19:19.5)cm]
ending with a WS row, shape shoulder.

SHAPE SHOULDER

Bind off 3 (3:4:4:4) sts at beg of next and foll alt
row. Purl 1 row.
Bind off 4 (4:4:4:5) sts at beg of next and foll alt
row.
Bind off rem 4 (5:4:5:4) sts.
Rejoin yarn at inner edge of sts on spare needle,
bind off 21 sts at center, work to end. Work from
**, reversing all shapings.

FRONT NECK FACING

With RS facing, using US 3 (3.25mm) needles,
pick up 58 sts from front neck, beg with a WS row,
work 3 rows st st. Change to US 5 (3.75mm)
needles.
Next row: Inc 10 sts evenly across row. 68 sts.
Work 3 rows more st st.
Change to US 6 (4mm) needles, inc 10 sts evenly
across first row, work 3 rows more in st st. Bind off
loosely over 78 sts.

BACK NECK FACING

Work as for front neck facing.

Crochet Insert

Using US D3 (3.25mm) crochet hook, make 130 (144:158:165:172) ch loosely.

Foundation row: 1 dc into 3rd ch from hook, * 2 ch, miss 2 ch, 1 sc into next ch, [make picot by working 3 ch, then 1 sl st into first of these ch] work 2nd sc into same ch as sc before picot, 2 ch, miss 2 ch, 1 dc into each of next 2 ch, rep. from * to end, turn.

Row 1: 1 sc between 2 dc of previous row, * 6 ch, 1 sc into ch space before the 2 dc, 1 ch, 1 sc into ch space after the 2 dc, rep from * ending with 1 ch, 1 sc into turning ch of previous row, turn.

Row 2: 1 sc into first st, * [3 dc, 2 ch, 3 dc] into the 6 ch, 1 sc into ch between 2 sc, rep from * to end, turn.

Row 3: 1 dc into first st, * 3 ch, [1 sc, 1 picot, 1 sc] into ch space between groups of 3 dc, 3 ch, 2 dc into sc, rep from * to end, turn.

These 3 rows form the pattern for inset.

Rep these 3 rows once more.

Change to US E4 (3.75mm) hook and work 6 rows in patt.

Change to US F5 (4mm) hook and cont until work measures 6 in. (15cm), ending with Row 3. Fasten off. Join crochet piece at narrow edges.

Using US D3 (3.25mm) hook work round cast-on

SINGLE CROCHET

Insert hook into stitch indicated, wrap the yarn around from back to front, and draw yarn through the stitch to make 2 loops

Wrap the yarn around from back to front and draw the yarn through the two loops on the hook

DOUBLE CROCHET

Pass yarn round hook, miss 2 ch, insert hook under 2 top threads of 3rd chain, pull a loop through.

Pass yarn round hook, pull loop through rem 2 loops.

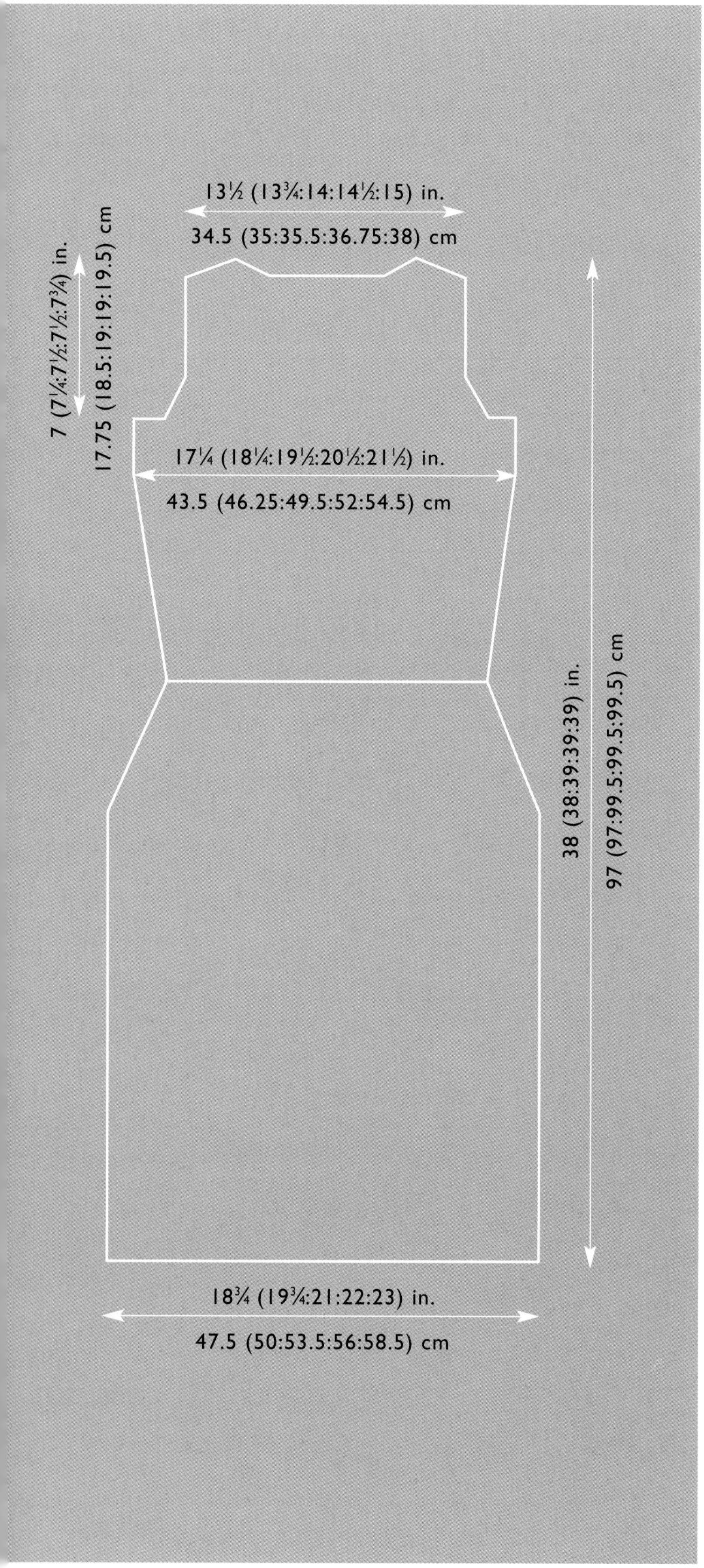

The schematic diagram shows the following measurements:

13½ (13¾:14:14½:15) in.
34.5 (35:35.5:36.75:38) cm

7 (7¼:7½:7½:7¾) in.
17.75 (18.5:19:19:19.5) cm

17¼ (18¼:19½:20½:21½) in.
43.5 (46.25:49.5:52:54.5) cm

38 (38:39:39:39) in.
97 (97:99.5:99.5:99.5) cm

18¾ (19¾:21:22:23) in.
47.5 (50:53.5:56:58.5) cm

edge as follows: Join yarn at seam, make 1 sc, 3 ch, 1 slip st into first of these ch [one picot], * 2 sc into next space, 2 sc into next space, 1 sc and one picot between 2 dc of last row, rep from * to end.

Finishing

Press all parts with a warm iron over a damp cloth. Sew side and shoulder seams of top. Turn neck facing to inside and slip stitch neatly in place. Join side seams of skirt. Turn up hem and slip stitch neatly. Sew crochet inset to top and skirt, placing shaped edges above the two rows in garter stitch. Stitch together along side seam.
Using US D3 (3.25mm) crochet hook work round armholes as follows:
Work 1 row in sc, turn, and with WS facing:
Next row: 2 sc, * 1 picot, 5 sc, rep from * to last 2 sts, work 2 sc.
Work round other armhole the same.

Sophia

You'll wonder how you ever did without this luxurious lacy cardigan. Whether you wear it as a twin set (see page 61), or on its own over a dress, you're bound to enjoy its effortless chic.

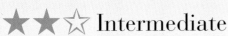 Intermediate

SIZES

	XS	S	M	L	XL	
To fit bust	32	34	36	38	40	in.
	81	86	91	97	102	cm

See diagram on page 56 for actual measurements.

YARN

8 (8:9:9:10) x 1¾ oz. (50g) balls of Rowan Cashsoft DK in Bella Donna 502

NEEDLES

Pair each of US 3 (3.25mm) and US 6 (4mm) needles
Stitch holders and markers

NOTIONS

8 buttons

GAUGE

22 sts and 30 rows to 4 in. (10cm) measured over pattern using US 6 (4mm) needles. Change needle size if necessary to obtain this gauge.

ABBREVIATIONS

See page 12.

STITCHES

1 x 1 rib
Stockinette stitch

CHARTS

Chart 1

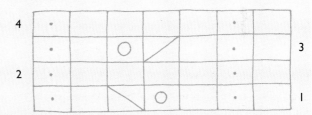

Chart 2

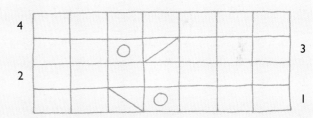

Key

	st st		ssk
	reverse st st		k2tog
	yo		

Note: Charts are read from right to left on RS rows and from left to right on WS rows.
After decreasing at armhole, omit zigzag stripe at side edges if it occurs on last 2 sts.

Back

Using smaller needles, cast on 90 (96:102:108:114) sts and refer to Chart 1 and repeat the 4 rows until work measures 1¼ in. (3cm), ending on a WS row. Center chart as follows:

RS rows: Work the last 1 (4:2:4:2) sts of chart, repeat the 11 sts 8 (8:9:9:10) times, work the first 1 (4:1:5:2) sts.

WS rows: Work the last 1 (4:1:5:2) sts, repeat the 11 sts 8 (8:9:9:10) times, work the first 1 (4:2:4:2) sts.

Change to larger needles and refer to Chart 2, centering chart as for Chart 1 and beg on next row after Chart 1 finished, ie if you finished Chart 1 on Row 2, beg Chart 2 on Row 3, if you finished Chart 1 on Row 4, beg Chart 2 on Row 1, so that lacy zigzag is correct.

Cont in patt as set until work measures 12 (12:12:11½:12) in. [30.5 (30.5:30.5:29.25:30.5)cm] from cast-on edge, ending on a WS row.

SHAPE ARMHOLE

Bind off 5 (5:5:6:6) sts at beg of next 2 rows. Then dec 1 st at both ends of next and every foll alt row 4 (4:7:8:10) times in all, keeping patt correct as set. 72 (78:78:80:82) sts. Continue in patt as set until work measures 19 (19:19½:19½:20) in. [48.25 (48.25:49.5:49.5:50.75)cm] from cast-on edge, ending on a WS row.

SHAPE SHOULDER AND NECK

Next row (RS): Work 24 (27:26:27:27) sts, place center 24 (24:26:26:28) sts on holder, join a second ball of yarn and work to end. Working both sides at the same time, dec 1 st at both neck edges on next and foll alt row.

At the same time work and place 7 (8:8:8:8) sts on holder at armhole edge on next row (for left back neck it will be foll row), and 7 (8:8:8:8) sts on foll alt row. Bind off over all 22 (25:24:25:25) sts.

Left Front

Using smaller needles, cast on 45 (48:51:54:57) sts and refer to Chart 1 and repeat the 4 rows until work measures 1¼ in. (3cm) ending on a WS row. Center chart as follows:

RS rows: Work the last 1 (4:2:4:2) sts of chart, repeat the 11 sts 4 (4:4:4:5) times, work the first 0 (0:5:6:0) sts (for size L, substitute rib instead of lacy zigzag on final st).

WS rows: Work the last 0 (0:5:6:0) sts, repeat the 11 sts 4 (4:4:4:5) times, work the first 1 (4:2:4:2) sts

Change to larger needles and refer to Chart 2, centering chart as for Chart 1 and beg on next row after Chart 1 finished as before.

Cont in patt as set until work measures 12 (12:12:11½:12) in. [30.5 (30.5:30.5:29.25:30.5)cm] from cast-on edge, ending on a WS row.

SHAPE ARMHOLE

Bind off 5 (5:5:6:6) sts at beg of next row. Work 1 row. Then dec 1 st at beg of next and every foll alt row 4 (4:7:8:10) times in all, keeping patt correct as set. 36 (39:39:40:41) sts. Cont in patt as set until work measures 17 (17:17½:17½:18) in. [43 (43:44.5:44.5:45.75)cm] from cast-on edge, ending on a WS row.

SHAPE NECK

Work and place 7 (7:8:8:9) sts at beg of next row on holder, then dec 1 st at neck edge on next and every foll alt row 7 times.

Cont until work measures 19 (19:19½:19½:20) in. [48.25 (48.25:49.5:49.5:50.75)cm] from cast-on edge, ending on a WS row.

SHAPE SHOULDER

Work and place 7 (8:8:8:8) sts on holder at armhole edge. Work 1 row.
Work and place 7 (8:8:8:8) sts on holder at armhole edge. Work 1 row.
Bind off over all 22 (25:24:25:25) sts.

Right Front

Work as for Left Front, reversing all shapings and centering charts as follows:

RS rows: Work the last 0 (0:5:6:0) sts, repeat the 11 sts 4 (4:4:4:5) times, work the first 1 (4:2:4:2) sts.

WS rows: Work the last 1 (4:2:4:2) sts of chart, repeat the 11 sts 4 (4:4:4:5) times, work the first 0 (0:5:6:0) sts (for L size, substitute rib instead of lacy zigzag on final st).

Sleeves

Using smaller needles, cast on 46 (46:46:50:50) sts and refer to Chart 1 and repeat the 4 rows until work measures 1¼ in. (3cm), ending on a WS row. Center chart as follows:

RS rows: Work the last 1 (1:1:3:3) sts of chart, repeat the 11 sts 4 times, work the first 1 (1:1:3:3) sts.

WS rows: Work the last 1 (1:1:3:3) sts of chart, repeat the 11 sts 4 times, work the first 1 (1:1:3:3) sts.

Change to larger needles and refer to Chart 2, centering chart as for Chart 1 and beg on next row after Chart 1 finished as before.

At the same time inc as follows, keeping patt correct as set.

XS 1 st at both ends of every 16th row 7 times. 60 sts.

S 1 st at both ends of every 14th row 8 times. 62 sts.

M 1 st at both ends of every 10th row 5 times, then every 11th row 6 times. 68 sts.

L 1 st at both ends of every 10th row 5 times, then every 11th row 6 times. 72 sts.

XL 1 st at both ends of every 8th row once, then every 9th row 12 times. 76 sts.

Cont as set until work measures 18 (18:18½: 18½:18½) in. [45.75 (45.75:47.5:47.5:47.5)cm] from cast-on edge, ending on a WS row.

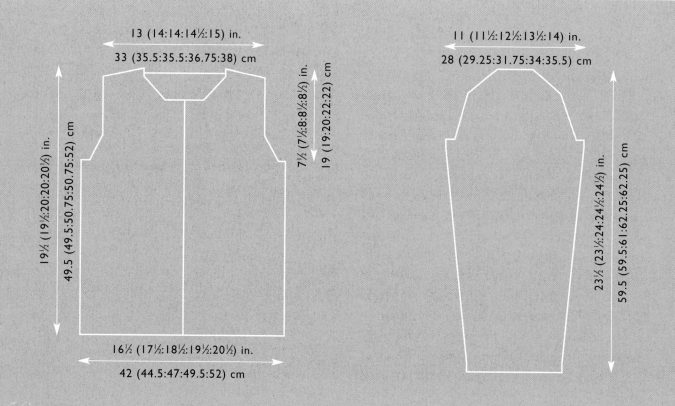

SHAPE SLEEVE CAP

Bind off 5 (5:5:6:6) sts at beg of next 2 rows. Then dec 1 st at both ends of next, then every foll alt row 0 (0:7:3:9) times, then every 3rd row 5 (9:7:11:7) times, then every 4th row 5 (2:0:0:0) times. 28 (28:28:30:30) sts.
Bind off 3 sts at beg of next 4 rows. Bind off rem 16 (16:16:18:18) sts.

Finishing

Join shoulder seams.
Set in sleeves placing any fullness evenly over top of sleeve cap and aligning zigzag stripes where possible. Sew side and sleeve seams in one line.

BUTTON BAND

Using smaller needles, cast on 6 sts and work in k1, p1 rib until band fits snugly when stretched slightly. Attach the band as you knit to ensure it fits well, and leave live st on holder. Mark and attach position of 7 buttons: the first ½ in. (1cm) from the bottom edge, the seventh 2 in. (5cm) from the top edge and the rest spaced evenly between.

BUTTONHOLE BAND

Work as for button band, inserting buttonholes on RS rows as follows:
Work 3 sts, join a second ball of yarn and work to end. Working both sides at the same time, work a further 2 rows, then work across all 6 sts on foll row.

NECKBAND

Using smaller needles, with RS facing, starting at right center front, pick up and k6 sts from buttonhole band holder, 7 (7:8:8:9) sts from holder at right front neck edge, 16 sts up to shoulder, k2 sts at right back neck edge, 24 (24:26:26:28) sts from holder at center back, k2 sts at left back neck edge, 16 sts down left neck edge, 7 (7:8:8:9) sts from holder at left front neck edge and k6 sts from button band holder. 86 (86:90:90:94) sts. Work ¾ in. (2cm) in k1, p1 rib, working 8th buttonhole on 2nd row of rib (RS row) as follows:
Work 3 sts, bind off 2 sts, work to end of row. Cast on these 2 sts when you come to them on foll row. Bind off in rib.

Katherine

Great as a twin set with the cardigan on page 53, but also cuts the mustard under a tailored jacket. The lacy pattern is surprisingly easy to knit.

★★☆ Intermediate

SIZES

	XS	S	M	L	XL	
To fit bust	32	34	36	38	40	in.
	81	86	91	97	102	cm

See diagram on page 60 for actual measurements.

YARN

5 (5:6:6:7) × 1¾ oz. (50g) balls of Rowan Cashsoft DK in Bella Donna 502

NEEDLES

Pair each of US 3 (3.25mm) and US 6 (4mm) needles
Stitch holders
Markers

GAUGE

22 sts and 30 rows to 4 in. (10cm) measured over pattern using US 6 (4mm) needles. Change needle size if necessary to obtain correct gauge.

ABBREVIATIONS

See page 12.

STITCHES

1 x 1 rib
Stockinette stitch

CHARTS

Chart 1

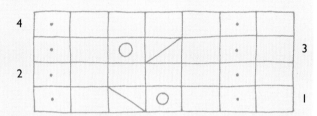

Chart 2

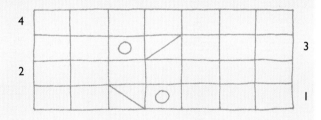

Key

	st st		ssk
	reverse st st		k2tog
	yo		

Note: Charts are read from right to left on RS rows and from left to right on WS rows.
After decreasing at armhole, omit zigzag stripe at side edges if it occurs on last 2 sts.

Back

Using smaller needles, cast on 88 (94:100:104: 110) sts. Refer to Chart 1 and repeat the 4 rows until work measures 1¼ in. (3cm), ending on a WS row. Center chart as follows:

RS rows: Work the last 2 (2:1:3:3) sts of chart, repeat the 7 sts 12 (13:14:14:15) times, work the first 2 (1:1:3:2) sts.

WS rows: Work the last 2 (1:1:3:2) sts, repeat the 7 sts 12 (13:14:14:15) times, work the first 2 (2:1:3:3) sts.

Change to larger needles and refer to Chart 2, centering chart as for Chart 1 and commencing on next row after Chart 1 finished, ie if you finished Chart 1 on Row 2, commence Chart 2 on Row 3, if you finished Chart 1 on Row 4, commence Chart 2 on Row 1, so that lacy zigzag will be correct. *At the same time* dec 1 st at both ends of next, then every foll 12th row twice. 82 (88:94:98:104) sts.

12½ (13:13½:14:14¼) in.
31.75 (33:34:35.5:36.5) cm

18½ (18½:19:19:19½) in.
47 (47:48.25:48.25:49.5) cm

7 (7:7½:7½:8) in.
17.75 (17.75:19:19:20) cm

16 (17:18:19:20) in.
40.5 (43:45.75:48.25:50.75) cm

Keep chart correct as you shape sweater. Work 1¼ in. (3cm) without shaping, then inc 1 st at both ends of next and then every foll 18th row twice, keeping patt correct as set. 88 (94:100:104:110) sts. Cont in patt as set until work measures 11½ in. (29.25cm) from cast-on edge, ending on a WS row.

SHAPE ARMHOLE

Bind off 4 (4:4:5:5) sts at beg of next 2 rows. Then dec 1 st at both ends of next and every foll alt row 6 (8:9:9:11) times in all, keeping patt correct as set. 68 (70:74:76:78) sts. Cont in patt until work measures work measures 18 (18:18½:18½:19) in. [45.75 (45.75:47:47:48.25)cm] from cast-on edge, ending on a WS row.

SHAPE SHOULDER AND NECK

Next row (RS): Work 20 (21:21:22:23) sts, place center 28 (28:32:32:32) sts on holder, join a second ball of yarn and work to end. Working both sides at the same time, dec 1 st at both neck edges on next and foll alt row.

At the same time work and place 6 (6:6:6:7) sts on holder at armhole edge on next row (for left back neck it will be foll row), and 6 (6:6:7:7) sts on foll alternate row. Bind off over whole 18 (19:19:20:21) sts.

Front

Work as for Back until work measures 16 (16:16½:16½:17) in. [40.5 (40.5:42:42:43)cm] from cast-on edge, ending on a WS row.

SHAPE NECK

Next row (RS): Work 26 (27:28:29:30) sts, place center 16 (16:18:18:18) sts on holder, join a second ball of yarn and work to end. Working both sides at the same time, dec 1 st at both neck edges on next and every row 4 (4:6:6:6) times, then every alt row 4 (4:3:3:3) times. 18 (19:19:20:21) sts. Cont until work measures 18 (18:18½:18½:19) in.

[45.75 (45.75:47:47:48.25)cm] from cast-on edge, ending on a WS row.

SHAPE SHOULDER

Work and place 6 (6:6:6:7) sts on holder at armhole edge. Work 1 row.
Work and place 6 (6:6:7:7) sts on holder at armhole edge. Work 1 row.
Bind off over whole 18 (19:19:20:21) sts.

Finishing

Join right shoulder seam.

COLLAR

Using smaller needles, with RS facing, starting at left shoulder seam, pick up and k16 sts down left neck edge 16 (16:18:18:18) sts from holder at center front, k16 sts up right neck edge, k2 sts down right back neck edge, 28 (28:32:32:32) sts from holder at center back and k2 sts up left back neck edge. 80 (80:86:86:86)sts. Work 2¼ in. (5.75cm) in k1, p1 rib. Bind off in rib.
Join other shoulder and neck seam.

CUFFS (WORK FOR EACH SLEEVE)

Using smaller needles, with RS facing, pick up and k96 (96:102:104:110) sts evenly around armhole edge and then bind off knitwise.
Sew side seams.

Ariane

This cropped jacket with a nautical flavor is knitted in brioche rib. Often called fisherman's rib, it's one of the easiest patterns to knit – creating a sweater that'll be a wow on the water.

★★☆ Intermediate

SIZES

	XS	S	M	L	XL	
To fit bust	32	34	36	38	40	in.
	81	86	91	97	102	cm

See diagram on page 64 for actual measurements.

YARN

11 (12:13:14:15) × 1¾ oz. (50g) balls of Rowan Wool/Cotton DK in French Navy 909 (A)
1 × 1¾ oz. (50g) ball of Rowan Wool/Cotton DK in Antique 900 (B)

NEEDLES

Pair each of US 3 (3.25mm) and US 6 (4mm) needles
Stitch holders

GAUGE

20 sts and 44 rows to 4 in. (10cm) measured over pattern using US 6 (4mm) needles. Change needle size if necessary to obtain this gauge.

ABBREVIATIONS

See page 12.

STITCHES

Brioche rib (multiple of 2 sts)
Foundation row: Knit.
Row 1: *K1, k1 below (insert needle through center of st below next st on needle and knit this in the usual way, slipping the stitch above off the needle at the same time); rep from * to last 2 sts, k2.
Rep Row 1 throughout.

Brioche rib

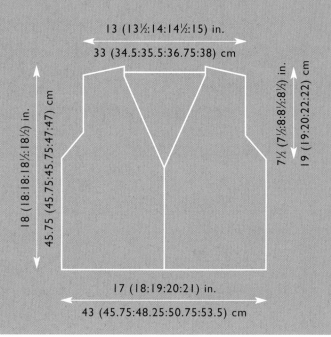

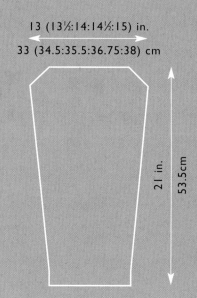

Back

Using smaller needles and A, cast on 84 (90:94:100:106) sts and, working in Brioche rib throughout, work 2 in. (5cm) ending on WS row. Change to larger needles and work in Brioche rib to end. Cont until work measures 10½ (10½:10:10:10) in. [26.5 (26.5:25.5:25.5:25.5)cm] from cast-on edge, ending on a WS row.

SHAPE ARMHOLE
Dec 1 st at both ends of next and every foll alt row 10 (11:12:14:16) times in all, keeping patt correct. 64 (68:70:72:74) sts.
Continue as set until work measures 17½ (17½:17½:18:18) in. [44.5 (44.5:44.5:45.75: 45.75)cm] from cast-on edge, ending on a WS row.

SHAPE SHOULDERS AND NECK
Next row: (RS) Work 20 (20:22:23:24) sts, bind off center 24 (24:26:26:26) sts on holder, join a second ball of yarn and work to end. Working both sides at the same time, dec 1 st at both neck edges on next and foll alt row.

At the same time work and place 6 (6:6:7:7) sts on holder at armhole edge on next row (for left back neck it will be foll row), and 6 (7:7:7:7) sts on foll alt row. Bind off over whole 18 (20:20:21:22) sts.

Left Front

Using smaller needles and A, cast on 40 (44:46:50:54) sts and working in Brioche rib throughout, work 2 in. (5cm) ending on WS row. Change to larger needles and work in Brioche rib to end. Cont until work measures 10½ (10½:10:10:10) in. [26.5 (26.5:25.5:25.5:25.5)cm] from cast-on edge, ending on a WS row.

SHAPE ARMHOLE
Dec 1 st at beg of next and every foll alt row 10 (11:12:14:16) times in all, keeping patt correct. 30 (33:34:36:38) sts. Cont until work measures 17½ (17½:17½:18:18) in. [44.5 (44.5:44.5: 45.75:45.75)cm] from cast-on edge, ending on a WS row.

SHAPE SHOULDERS

Work and place 6 (6:6:7:7) sts on holder at armhole edge, work to end of row. Work 1 row. Work and place 6 (7:7:7:7) sts on holder at armhole edge, work to end of row. Work 1 row. Work and place 6 (7:7:7:8) sts on holder at armhole edge, work to end of row. Leave remaining 12 (13:14:15:16) sts on holder.

Right Front

As Left Front, reversing all shapings.
Note: Both fronts should end on same number of rows (ie a WS row) as Right Front shoulder shaping is done on WS rows.

Sleeves

Using smaller needles and A, cast on 44 (44:44:48:48) sts and working in Brioche rib throughout, work 1½ in. (3.75cm), ending on a WS row. Change to larger needles and cont in Brioche rib to end, inc as follows:

XS 1 st at both ends of Row 13, then every foll 18th row 10 times in all. 64 sts.

S 1 st at both ends of Row 15, then every foll 14th row 12 times in all. 68 sts.

M 1 st at both ends of Row 1, then every foll 14th row 13 times in all. 70 sts.

L 1 st at both ends of Row 9, then every foll 14th row 12 times in all. 72 sts.

XL 1 st at both ends of Row 17, then every foll 12th row 13 times in all. 74 sts.

Cont as set until work measures 19½ (19:18¾: 18½:18¼) in. [49.5 (48.25:47.5:47:46.25)cm].

SHAPE TOP OF SLEEVE

Dec 1 st at both ends of next and every foll alt row 10 (11:12:14:16) times in all, keeping patt correct. Bind off rem 44 (46:46:44:42) sts in patt.

Finishing

Join shoulder seams.

COLLAR

With RS of fronts facing and with collars folded back, using A and larger needles, pick up and cont in brioche patt 12 (13:14:15:16) sts from holder at top of Left Front, then with WS of back facing, 4 sts down back neck edge, 24 (24:26:26:26) sts from center back, 4 sts up other side of back neck edge, then with RS of Right Front facing, 12 (13:14:15:16) sts from holder at top of right front. 56 (58:62:64:66) sts. Work a further 8 in. (20cm) in brioche pattern keeping patt correct as set. Bind off. Set in sleeves placing any fullness evenly over top of sleeve cap. Sew side and sleeve seams in one line. Using B, work blanket stitch around cuff edges. Then starting at left side seam, work blanket stitch evenly along bottom edge of Back, Right Front, up center Right Front edge, around edge of collar, down center Left Front edge and along bottom Left Front to finish at starting point.

BLANKET STITCH

Bring a needle threaded with yarn out from back to front at the center of a knitted stitch 2 sts up from edge. *Insert the needle at the center of a stitch to the right and two rows up, and out at the bottom edge, catching the loop of yarn two rows below. Repeat from *.

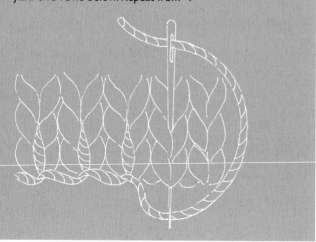

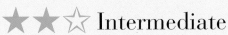

Chiquita

A toe in the water for would-be lace knitters, this classic sweater has a lacy rib at the hem, cuffs and collar. Embellish the look with pompom ties to add a retro feel, or fasten with a pin.

★★☆ Intermediate

SIZES

	XS	S	M	L	XL	
To fit bust	32	34	36	38	40	in.
	81	86	91	97	102	cm

See diagram on page 70 for actual measurements.

YARN

8 (9:9:10:10) × 1¾ oz. (50g) balls of Artesano Inca Cloud Alpaca in Teal 61

NEEDLES

Pair each of US 3 (3.25mm) and US 5 (3.75mm) needles
US 3 (3.25mm) circular needle
Cable needle
US 5 (3.75mm) crochet hook
Stitch holders

GAUGE

24 sts and 32 rows to 4 in. (10cm) measured over stockinette stitch, using US 5 (3.75mm) needles. Change needle size if necessary to obtain this gauge.

ABBREVIATIONS

See page 12.

STITCHES

Lacy cable rib (multiple of 7 + 6)

Row 1 (RS): K1, *k2tog, yo twice, ssk, k3; rep from * to last 5 sts, k2tog, yo twice, ssk, k1.

Row 2: K1, *k1, k1 tbl, k2, p3; rep from * to last 5 sts, k1, k1 tbl, k2, p1.

Row 3: K1, *k2tog, yo twice, ssk, skip next 2 sts and knit 3rd st, then knit 2nd st, then knit first st, then slip all 3 sts from needle tog; rep from * ending last repeat, k2tog, yo twice, ssk, k1.

Row 4: K1, *k1, k1 tbl, k2, p3; rep from * to last 5 sts, k1, k1 tbl, k2, p1.

Rep these 4 rows.

Stockinette stitch

Back

Using smaller needles, cast on 97 (104:111:118:125) sts and work 20 rows in Lacy Cable Rib. Change to larger needles and work in st st to end. Cont until work measures 11½ in. (29.25cm) from cast-on edge, ending on a WS row.

SHAPE ARMHOLE

Bind off 5 (5:5:6:6) sts at beg of next 2 rows. Then dec 1 st at both ends of next and every foll alt row 4 (6:8:9:11) times. 79 (82:85:88:91) sts. Cont until work measures 18½ (18½:19:19:19½) in. [47 (47:48.25:48.25:49.5)cm] from cast-on edge, ending on a WS row.

SHAPE NECK AND SHOULDER

Next row: Work 23 (24:25:26:27) sts, place center 33 (34:35:36:37) sts on holder, join a second ball of yarn and work to end. Working both sides at the same time, dec 1 st at both neck edges on next and foll alt row.

At the same time work and place 7 (7:7:8:8) sts on holder at armhole edge on next row (for left back neck it will be on foll row), and 7 (7:8:8:8) sts on foll alt row. Bind off over all 21 (22:23:24:25) sts.

Front

Work as for Back up to and including armhole shaping. *At the same time* when work measures 11½ (11½:12:12:12½) in. [29.25 (29.25:30.5:30.5:31.75)cm] from cast-on edge, ending on WS row, split neck.

SPLIT NECK

Work to center point, (for XS, M and XL sizes, bind off center st), join a second ball of yarn and work to end. Working both sides at the same time, cont as set until work measures 16½ (16½:17:17:17½) in. [42 (42:43:43:44.5)cm] from cast-on edge, ending on a WS row (RS row for other side).

SHAPE NECKLINE

Next row: Work 31 (32:33:34:35) sts, place center 8 (9:9:10:10) sts on holder. Then dec 1 st at both neck edges on next and every foll row 10 times. Working both sides at the same time, cont as set until work measures 18½ (18½:19:19:19½) in. [47 (47:48.25:48.25: 49.5)cm] from cast-on edge, ending on a WS row.

SHAPE SHOULDERS

Work and place 7 (7:7:8:8) sts on holder at armhole edge on next row (for left back neck it will be foll row), then work and place 7 (7:8:8:8) sts on foll alt row. Bind off over all 21 (22:23:24:25) sts.

Sleeves

Using smaller needles, cast on 48 (48:48:55:55) sts and work 20 rows in Lacy Cable Rib. Change to larger needles and work in st st to end, inc as follows:

XS 1 st at both ends of every 12th row 9 times. 66 sts.

S 1 st at both ends of every 9th row twice, then every 10th row 9 times. 70 sts.

M 1 st at both ends of every 8th row 14 times. 76 sts.

L 1 st at both ends of every 8th row 5 times, then every 9th row 8 times. 81 sts.

XL 1 st at both ends of every 7th row 8 times, then every 8th row 7 times. 85 sts.

Cont until work measures 18 (18:18½:18½:18½) in. [45.75 (45.75:47:47:47)cm] from cast-on edge, ending on a WS row.

SHAPE SLEEVE CAP

Bind off 5 (5:5:6:6) sts at beg of next 2 rows. Then dec as follows:

XS 1 st at both ends of every 3rd row 8 times, then every alt row 7 times. 26 sts.

S 1 st at both ends of every 3rd row 4 times, then every alt row 13 times. 26 sts.

M 1 st at both ends every alt row 18 times, then every row twice. 26 sts.
L 1 st at both ends of every 3rd row twice, then every alt row 18 times. 29 sts.
XL 1 st at both ends of every alt row 20 times, then every row twice. 29 sts
Bind off 3 sts at beg of next 4 rows. Bind off rem 14 (14:14:17:17) sts.

Finishing

Join shoulder seams.

NECKBAND

With RS facing and using US 3 (3.25mm) circular needle, starting at right center front neck edge, pick up and k8 (9:9:10:10) sts from holder, k19 (17:20:19:18) sts up neck edge to shoulder seam, 2 sts down back neck edge, 33 (34:35:36:37) sts from holder at center back, 2 sts up other side neck edge, k18 (17:20:18:18) sts down left neck edge and k8 (9:9:10:10) sts from holder at center left front. 90 (90:90:97:97) sts.

Next row (working back and forth): K2, *yo, k2tog; rep from * to end. For L and XL sizes end k1. Then cont in lacy cable rib for a further 2 in. (5cm) and then bind off.

FRONT SLIT

Using smaller needles, with RS facing, starting at top of left collar, pick up and k44 sts to bottom of opening, pick up and k1 st in center and then k44 sts up other side to top of right collar. 89 sts.
Bind off knitwise.
Set in sleeves, easing any fullness evenly across top of cap. Sew side and sleeve seams in one line.

POMPOMS

Make two pompoms (see opposite). Using crochet hook and doubled yarn make chain cord 36 in. (92cm) long, thread through row of eyelets on collar, then attach pompom at each end.

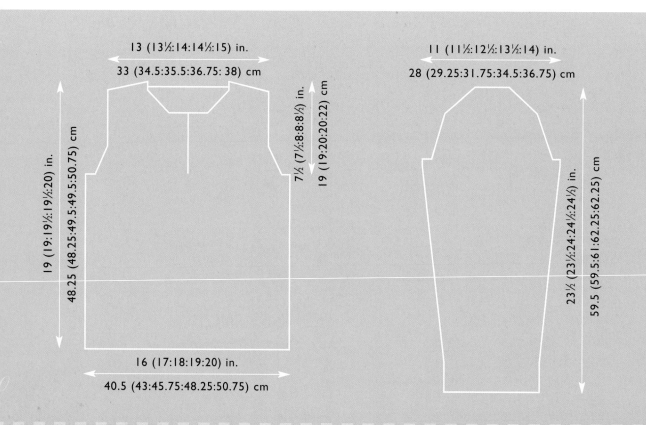

13 (13½:14:14½:15) in.
33 (34.5:35.5:36.75: 38) cm

7½ (7½:8:8:8½) in.
19 (19:20:20:22) cm

19 (19:19½:19½:20) in.
48.25 (48.25:49.5:49.5:50.75) cm

16 (17:18:19:20) in.
40.5 (43:45.75:48.25:50.75) cm

11 (11½:12½:13½:14) in.
28 (29.25:31.75:34.5:36.75) cm

23½ (23½:24:24½:24½) in.
59.5 (59.5:61:62.25:62.25) cm

POMPOMS

Cut 2 cardboard circles, 2 in. (5cm) across (pompoms will measure 1½ in. (3.75cm) across). Cut a ¾ in. (2cm) hole in center of each circle. Cut a small wedge of each circle away to make it easier to wrap the yarn.

Place a tie strand between the 2 circles before wrapping. Wrap yarn around both circles many times; the more wraps the thicker the pompom, so wrap densely. Insert scissors between the circles and carefully cut around outer edges to release yarn. Knot the tie strand tightly around center of yarn lengths. Gently ease cardboard from the pompom.

Cut 2 cardboard circles 1¼ in. (3cm) wide with pinpoint center holes. Place pompom between circles. Insert long embroidery needle through pinpoint holes in cardboard and center of pompom. Trim around circles to even pompom.

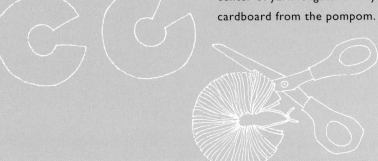

Melissa

This off-the-shoulder fitted top is wonderfully versatile. If stripes are not "you", work the hem, cuffs, and neck in a solid contrast color or glam it up for the evening with a classy hat.

★☆☆ Beginner

SIZES

	XS	S	M	L	XL	
To fit bust	32	34	36	38	40	in.
	81	86	91	97	102	cm

See diagram on page 74 for actual measurements.

YARN

5 (6:7:7:8) × 1¾ oz. (50g) balls of Artesano Inca Cloud Alpaca in Baby Pink 95 (A)

1 (2:2:2:2) × 1¾ oz. (50g) balls of Artesano Inca Cloud Alpaca in Black 12 (B)

NEEDLES

Pair each of US 3 (3.25mm) and US 5 (3.75mm) needles
US 3 (3.25mm) circular needle

GAUGE

24 sts and 32 rows to 4 in. (10cm) measured over stockinette stitch using US 5 (3.75mm) needles. Change needle size if necessary to obtain this gauge.

ABBREVIATIONS

See page 12.

STITCHES

Garter stitch
Stockinette stitch

Back and Front

Using smaller needles and A, cast on 96 (102:108:114:120) sts and work 14 rows in garter st as follows:

Rows 1, 2, 7, 8, 9 and 10: Work in A.
Rows 3, 4, 5, 6, 11, 12, 13 and 14: Work in B.
Change to larger needles and work to end in st st in A, dec 1 st at both ends of next and every foll 5th (7th:9th:11th:13th) row 3 times in all.
88 (96:102:108:114) sts.
Work 8 rows without shaping, then inc 1 st at both ends of next and every foll 18th (15th:17th:15th:13th) row 3 times in all.
96 (102:108:114:120) sts. Cont until work measures 10 (10¼:10¾:10¾:10¾) in.
[25.5 (26:27.25:27.25:27.25)cm] from cast-on edge, ending on a WS row.

SHAPE ARMHOLE

Bind off 5 (5:5:6:6) sts at beg of next 2 rows.
Then dec 1 st at both ends of every alt row 0 (4:4:0:2) times, then every 3rd row 4 (6:6:10:10) times, then every 4th row 3 (0:0:0:0) times.
72 (72:78:82:84) sts.

WORK NECKLINE

At the same time starting on Row 15 (17:17:19:23) of armhole decreases, work neckline as follows: Work 12 (12:12:15:15) sts as set, k2tog, bind off the next 50 (50:56:56:58) sts and place the rem 14 (14:14:17:17) sts on holder. Working side of neck separately, dec 1 st at neck edge as set on every row 10 (10:10:12:12) times in all, working armhole decs simultaneously. Bind off last st. Work other side to match.

Sleeves

Using smaller needles and A cast on 54 (54:54:58:58) sts and work 14 rows in garter st as follows:

Rows 1, 2, 7, 8, 9 and 10: Work in A.
Rows 3, 4, 5, 6, 11, 12, 13 and 14: Work in B Change to larger needles and work to end in st st in A, inc as follows:

XS 1 st at both ends of every 12th row twice, then every 13th row 4 times. 66 sts.
S 1 st at both ends of every 10th row once, then every 11th row 6 times. 68 sts.
M 1 st at both ends of every 8th row 5 times, then every 9th row 4 times. 72 sts.
L 1 st at both ends of every 9th row 4 times, then every 10 row 4 times. 74 sts.
XL 1 st at both ends of every 7th row 4 times, then every 8th row 6 times. 78 sts.
Cont until work measures 12 in. (30.5cm) from cast-on edge.

SHAPE SLEEVE CAP

Bind off 5 (5:5:6:6) sts at beg of next 2 rows. Then dec 1 st at both ends of every 3rd row 0 (0:0:4:6) times, then every alt row 11 (13:12:9:8) times, then every row 2 (0:2:0:0) times. 30 (32:34:36:38) sts. Bind off.

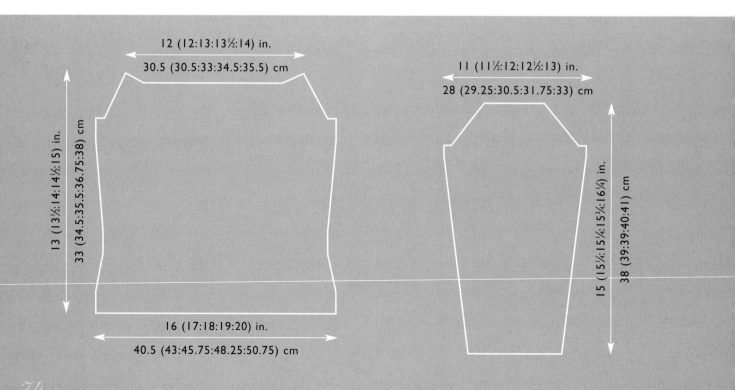

12 (12:13:13½:14) in.
30.5 (30.5:33:34.5:35.5) cm

13 (13½:14:14½:15) in.
33 (34.5:35.5:36.75:38) cm

16 (17:18:19:20) in.
40.5 (43:45.75:48.25:50.75) cm

11 (11½:12:12½:13) in.
28 (29.25:30.5:31.75:33) cm

15 (15¼:15¼:15¾:16¼) in.
38 (39:39:40:41) cm

Finishing

Join raglan seams.
Sew side and sleeve seams in one line.

COLLAR

Using circular needle and B, starting at top of
left sleeve, with RS facing, pick up and k30
(32:34:36:38) sts along top edge of sleeve,
66 (66:76:76:78) sts across front, k30
(32:34:36:38) sts along top edge of other sleeve,
and 66 (66:76:76:78) sts across back.
192 (196:220:224:232) sts. Join and work 37 rows
in the round in garter st as follows:

Round 1: Purl in B.
Round 2: Knit in B.
Round 3: Purl in B.
Round 4: Knit in A.
Round 5: Purl in A.
Round 6: Knit in A.
Round 7: Purl in A.
Round 8: Knit in B.
Rep these 8 rounds 3 more times then work
Rounds 1–5 and then bind off in A.

Elizabeth

Get speedy results with this tie-fronted vest. Unwind with your knitting on a Friday evening and you'll be snuggling up in this funky vest before the weekend is through.

 ## Beginner

SIZES

	XS	S	M	L	XL	
To fit bust	32	34	36	38	40	in.
	81	86	91	97	101	cm

See diagram on page 79 for actual measurements.

YARN
5 (5:6:6:7) x 3½ oz. (100g) balls of Sirdar Bigga in Tulip 687

NEEDLES
Pair each of US 17 (12mm) and US 19 (15mm) needles
Stitch holders

GAUGE
6 sts and 9 rows to 4 in. (10cm) measured over stockinette stitch using US 19 (15mm) needles. Change needle size if necessary to obtain this gauge.

ABBREVIATIONS
See page 12.

STITCHES
Garter stitch
Stockinette stitch

Back

Using smaller needles cast on 24 (25:28:30:31) sts and work 4 rows in garter st. Change to larger needles and work in st st to end. Cont until work measures 8 in. (20cm) from cast-on edge, ending on a WS row.

SHAPE ARMHOLE
Dec 1 st at both ends of next and foll alt rows 2 (2:3:3:3) times in all. 20 (21:22:24:25) sts. Cont as set until work measures 15 (15:15:15½:15½) in. [38 (38:38:39.5:39.5)cm] from cast-on edge, ending on a WS row.

SHAPE SHOULDER
Work and place 3 sts on holder at beg of next 2 rows. Then work and place 3 (3:3:4:4) sts on holder at beg of foll 2 rows. Bind off over all 20 (21:22:24:25) sts.

Left Front

Using smaller needles cast on 81 (82:85:87:88) sts and work 4 rows in garter st, binding off 57 sts at beg of final row 24 (25:28:30:31) sts. Change to larger needles and cont in st st to end, dec as follows:

XS 1 st at neck edge on next, then every foll row 4 times, then every foll alt row 11 times. 6 sts.

S 1 st at neck edge on next, then every foll row 6 times, then every foll alt row 10 times. 6 sts.

M 1 st at neck edge on next, then every foll row 10 times, then every foll alt row 8 times. 6 sts.

L 1 st at neck edge on next, then every foll row 11 times, then every foll alt row 8 times. 7 sts.

XL 1 st at neck edge on next, then every foll row 13 times, then every foll alt rows 7 times. 7 sts.

At the same time when work measures 8 in. (20cm) from cast-on edge, ending on WS row, shape armhole.

SHAPE ARMHOLE

Dec 1 st at armhole edge on next and foll alt rows 2 (2:3:3:3) times in all.

Cont until work measures 15 (15:15:15½:15½) in. [38 (38:38:39.5:39.5)cm] from cast-on edge, ending on a WS row.

SHAPE SHOULDER

Work and place 3 sts on holder at beg of next row. Work 1 row. Then work and place 3 (3:3:4:4) sts on holder at beg of next row. Bind off over all 6 (6:6:7:7) sts.

Right Front

Work as for Left Front reversing all shapings, casting off the 57 sts on first row of st st.

Finishing

Use mattress stitch for seams (see page 40). Join shoulder seams.

NECKBAND

Using smaller needles, with RS facing, starting at bottom right front (where bound-off sts for tie ends), pick up and k32 (32:32:34:34) sts to shoulder, 8 (9:10:10:11) sts across back neck and k32 (32:32:34:34) sts down left front neck edge to beg of tie. 72 (73:74:78:79) sts. Bind off knitwise.

ARMBANDS

Using smaller needles, with RS facing, pick up and k32 (32:32:34:34) sts evenly along armhole edge. Bind off knitwise.

Join side seams in one line leaving 1 in. (2.5cm) space (to fit tie) in left side seam directly above garter st. Stitch 1 in. (2.5cm) length of yarn (stitch at top and bottom to form loop on inside for tie) in same place on other side seam.

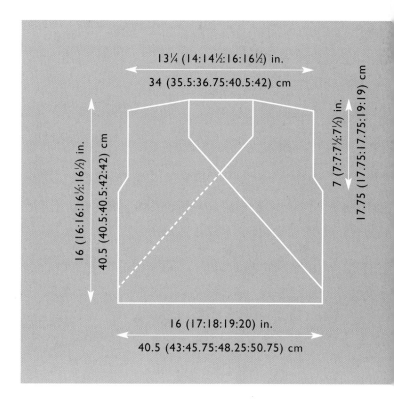

13¼ (14:14½:16:16½) in.
34 (35.5:36.75:40.5:42) cm

16 (16:16:16½:16½) in.
40.5 (40.5:40.5:42:42) cm

7 (7:7:7½:7½) in.
17.75 (17.75:17.75:19:19) cm

16 (17:18:19:20) in.
40.5 (43:45.75:48.25:50.75) cm

Rachel

*If you aren't yet up to the knot pattern of this fitted shawl collar
cardigan, work it in stockinette stitch and trim the cuffs, hem,
and collar with a couple of rows in the same color as the buttons.*

 Intermediate

SIZES

	XS	S	M	L	XL	
To fit bust	32	34	36	38	40	in.
	81	86	91	97	102	cm

See diagram on page 85 for actual measurements.

YARN

10 (11:12:13:14) × 1¾ oz. (50g) balls of Artesano Inca Cloud
Alpaca in Light Grey 09
Use yarn doubled throughout

NOTIONS

4 buttons

NEEDLES

Pair each of US 7 (4.5mm) and US 9 (5.5mm) needles
Stitch holders

GAUGE

16 sts and 22 rows to 4 in. (10cm) measured over knot
pattern using US 9 (5.5mm) needles. Change needle size if
necessary to obtain this gauge.

ABBREVIATIONS

See page 12.

STITCHES

1 × 1 rib

Knot pattern (multiple of 12 + 3)

Rows 1, 3 and 5: Knit.

Rows 2, 4 and 6: Purl.

Row 7: *K9, (p3tog, k3tog, p3tog) into next 3 sts ; rep from
* to last 3 sts, k3.

Rows 8, 10, 12 and 14: Purl.

Rows 9, 11 and 13: Knit.

Row 15: K3, *(p3tog, k3tog, p3tog) into next 3 sts, k9; rep
from * to end.

Row 16: Purl.

Repeat these 16 rows.

Back

Using smaller needles, cast on 61 (65:69:73:77) sts and work in 1 × 1 rib until work measures 2½ in. (6.25cm), ending on a WS row. Change to larger needles and refer to knot pattern, repeating the 16 rows to end. Center pattern on Rows 7 and 15 as follows:

XS

Row 7: K2, (p3tog, k3tog, p3tog) into next 3 sts, *k9, (p3tog, k3tog, p3tog) into next 3 sts; rep from * to last 8 sts, k8.

Row 15: K8, *(p3tog, k3tog, p3tog) into next 3 sts, k9; rep from * to last 5 sts, (p3tog, k3tog, p3tog) into next 3 sts, k2.

S

Row 7: K1, *k9, (p3tog, k3tog, p3tog) into next 3 sts; rep from * to last 4 sts, k4.

Row 15: K4, *(p3tog, k3tog, p3tog) into next 3 sts, k9; rep from * to last st, k1.

M

Row 7: (P3tog, k3tog, p3tog) into next 3 sts, *k9, (p3tog, k3tog, p3tog) into next 3 sts; rep from * to last 6 sts, k6.

Row 15: K6, *(p3tog, k3tog, p3tog) into next 3 sts, k9; rep from * to last 3 sts, (p3tog, k3tog, p3tog) into next three sts.

L

Row 7: K2, (p3tog, k3tog, p3tog) into next 3 sts, *k9, (p3tog, k3tog, p3tog) into next 3 sts; rep from * to last 8 sts, k8.

Row 15: K8, *(p3tog, k3tog, p3tog) into next 3 sts, k9; rep from * to last 5 sts, (p3tog, k3tog, p3tog) into next 3 sts, k2.

XL

Row 7: K1, *k9, (p3tog, k3tog, p3tog) into next 3 sts; rep from * to last 4 sts, k4.

Row 15: K4, *(p3tog, k3tog, p3tog) into next 3 sts, k9; rep from * to last st, k1.

At the same time, inc 1 st at both ends of Rows 11 and 25, incorporating the increased sts into pattern where appropriate. 65 (69:73:77:81) sts.

Cont in patt as set until work measures 11½ in. (29.25cm) from cast-on edge, ending on a WS row.

SHAPE ARMHOLE

Bind off 3 (3:3:4:4) sts at beg of next 2 rows. Then dec 1 st at both ends of next and every foll alt row 3 (4:5:5:6) times, keeping pattern correct as set. 53 (55:57:59:61) sts.

Cont until work measures 18½ (18½:19:19:19) in. [47 (47:48.25:48.25:48.25)cm] from cast-on edge, ending on a WS row.

SHAPE NECK AND SHOULDER

Next row: Work 17 (18:18:19:20) sts, place center 19 (19:21:21:21) sts on holder, join a second ball of yarn and work to end. Working both sides at the same time, dec 1 st at both neck edges on next and foll alt row.

At the same time work and place 5 (5:5:5:6) sts on holder at armhole edge on next row, (for left back neck it will be on foll row), and 5 (5:5:6:6) sts on foll alt row. Bind off over whole 15 (16:16:17:18) sts.

Left Front

Using smaller needles, cast on 35 (37:39:41:43) sts and work in 1 × 1 rib until work measures 2½ in. (6.25cm), ending on a WS row.

Change to larger needles and refer to knot pattern, repeating the 16 rows to end, leaving 9 sts for band on holder at end of first row. 26 (28:30:32:34) sts. Center pattern on Rows 7 and 15 as follows:

XS

Row 7: K2, (p3tog, k3tog, p3tog) into next 3 sts, k9, (p3tog, k3tog, p3tog) into next 3 sts, k9.

Row 15: K8, (p3tog, k3tog, p3tog) into next 3 sts, k9, (p3tog, k3tog, p3tog) into next 3 sts, k3.

S

Row 7: K1, *k9, (p3tog, k3tog, p3tog) into next 3 sts; rep from * to last 3 sts, k3.

Row 15: K4, *(p3tog, k3tog, p3tog) into next 3 sts, k9; rep from * end.

M

Row 7: (P3tog, k3tog, p3tog) into next 3 sts, *k9, (p3tog, k3tog, p3tog) into next 3 sts; rep from * to last 3 sts, k3.

Row 15: K6, *(p3tog, k3tog, p3tog) into next 3 sts, k9; rep from * to end.

L

Row 7: K2, (p3tog, k3tog, p3tog) into next 3 sts, *k9, (p3tog, k3tog, p3tog) into next 3 sts; rep from * to last 3 sts, k3.

Row 15: K8, *(p3tog, k3tog, p3tog) into next 3 sts, k9; rep from * to end.

XL

Row 7: K1, *k9, (p3tog, k3tog, p3tog) into next 3 sts; rep from * to last 9 sts, k9.

Row 15: K4, *(p3tog, k3tog, p3tog) into next 3 sts, k9; rep from * to last 6 sts, (p3tog, k3tog, p3tog) into next 3 sts, k3.

At the same time, inc 1 st at beg (armhole edge) of Rows 11 and 25 rows, incorporating the increased sts into pattern where appropriate.
28 (30, 32, 34, 36) sts.
Cont in patt as set until work measures 11 in. (28cm).

SHAPE NECKLINE

Dec 1 st at neck edge on next, then every foll 5th row 0 (0:5:5:5) times, then every foll 6th row 6 (6:2:2:2) times, keeping patt correct as set. 15 (16:16:17:18) sts.
At the same time when work measures 11½ in. (29.25cm) from cast-on edge, ending on a WS row, shape armhole.

SHAPE ARMHOLE

Bind off 3 (3:3:4:4) sts at beg of next row. Work 1 row. Then dec 1 st at beg of next and every foll alt row 3 (4:5:5:6) times, keeping pattern correct as set. Cont until work measures 18½ (18½:19:19:19) in. [47 (47:48.25:48.25:48.25)cm] from cast-on edge, ending on a WS row.

SHAPE SHOULDERS

Work and place 5 (5:5:5:6) sts on holder at armhole edge on next row (for left back neck it will be foll row), then work and place 5 (5:5:6:6) sts on foll alternate row. Bind off over whole 15 (16:16:17:18) sts.

Right Front

Using smaller needles, cast on 35 (37:39:41:43) sts and work in 1 × 1 rib until work measures 2½ in. (6.25cm), ending on a WS row.
At the same time when work measures ½ in. (1.25cm), from bottom edge ending on a WS row, work buttonhole.

BUTTONHOLE

Work 5 sts, join a second ball of yarn and work to end. Working both sides at the same time, work a further 3 rows, then work across all sts on foll row. Work to end as for Left Front, reversing all shapings and 9 sts for band.
Center patt as follows:

XS

Row 7: K9, (p3tog, k3tog, p3tog) into next 3 sts, k9, (p3tog, k3tog, p3tog) into next 3 sts, k2.

Row 15: K3, (p3tog, k3tog, p3tog) into next 3 sts, k9, (p3tog, k3tog, p3tog) into next 3 sts, k8.

S

Row 7: K3, *(p3tog, k3tog, p3tog) into next 3 sts, k9; rep from * to last st, k1.

Row 15: *K9, (p3tog, k3tog, p3tog) into next 3 sts; rep from * to last 4 sts, k4.

M

Row 7: K3, *(p3tog, k3tog, p3tog) into next 3 sts, k9; rep from * to last 3 sts, (p3tog, k3tog, p3tog) into next three sts.

Row 15: *K9, (p3tog, k3tog, p3tog) into next 3 sts; rep from * to last 6 sts, k6.

L

Row 7: K3, *(p3tog, k3tog, p3tog) into next 3 sts, k9; rep from * to last 5 sts, (p3tog, k3tog, p3tog) into next 3 sts, k2.

Row 15: *K9, (p3tog, k3tog, p3tog) into next 3 sts; rep from * to last 8 sts, k8.

XL

Row 7: K9, *(p3tog, k3tog, p3tog) into next 3 sts, k9; rep from * to last st, k1.

Row 15: K3, (p3tog, k3tog, p3tog) into next 3 sts, *k9, (p3tog, k3tog, p3tog) into next 3 sts; rep from * to last 4 sts, k4.

Sleeves

Using smaller needles, cast on 36 (36:36:38:38) sts and work in 1 × 1 rib until work measures 1½ in. (3.75cm). Change to larger needles and refer to knot pattern, repeating the 16 rows to end. Center pattern on Rows 7 and 15 as follows:

XS, S and M

Row 7: K2, (p3tog, k3tog, p3tog) into next 3 sts *k9, (p3tog, k3tog, p3tog) into next 3 sts; rep from * to last 7 sts, k7.

Row 15: K8, *(p3tog, k3tog, p3tog) into next 3 sts, k9; rep from * to last 5 sts, (p3tog, k3tog, p3tog) into next 3 sts, k2.

L and XL

Row 7: K3, (p3tog, k3tog, p3tog) into next 3 sts *k9, (p3tog, k3tog, p3tog) into next 3 sts; rep from * to last 8 sts, k8.

Row 15: *K9, (p3tog, k3tog, p3tog) into next 3 sts; rep from * to last 2 sts, k2.

At the same time inc 1 st at both ends of every 20th (16th:12th:10th:9th) row 4 (5:7:8:9) times. 44 (46:50:54:56) sts.

Keep the pattern correct as you increase. Continue until work measures 18 (18:18½:18½:18½) in. [45.75 (45.75:47:47:47)cm] from cast-on edge, ending on a WS row.

SHAPE SLEEVE CAP

Bind off 3 (3:3:4:4) sts at beg of next 2 rows. Then dec 1 st at both ends of every 3rd row 5 (3:0:2:0) times, then every alt row 5 (8:12:11:14) times, then every row 0 (0:1:0:0) times, keeping patt correct as set. Bind off 2 sts at beg of next 4 rows. Bind off rem 10 (10:10:12:12) sts.

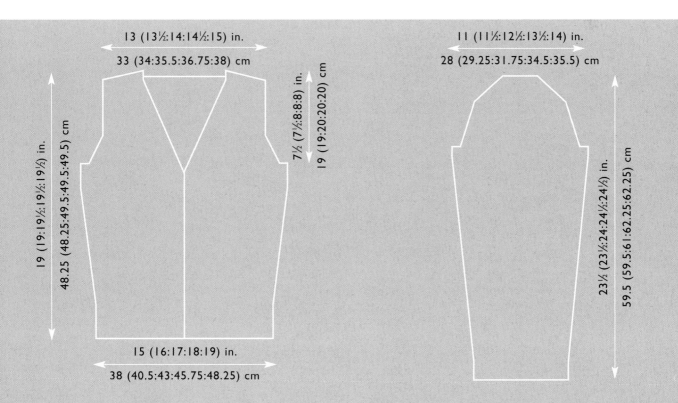

13 (13½:14:14½:15) in.
33 (34:35.5:36.75:38) cm

7½ (7½:8:8:8) in.
19 (19:20:20:20) cm

19 (19:19½:19½:19½) in.
48.25 (48.25:49.5:49.5:49.5) cm

15 (16:17:18:19) in.
38 (40.5:43:45.75:48.25) cm

11 (11½:12½:13½:14) in.
28 (29.25:31.75:34.5:35.5) cm

23½ (23½:24:24½:24½) in.
59.5 (59.5:61:62.25:62.25) cm

Finishing

Join shoulder seams.

BUTTON BAND

Using smaller needles, pick up 9 sts from holder at center left front and work in 1 × 1 rib to start of v-neck. Band should fit snugly when stretched slightly. Attach the band to Left Front as you knit to ensure it fits well, then leave sts on holder.

BUTTONHOLE BAND

As left band, inserting buttonholes on RS rows as before.

Mark position of 3 buttons: the 4th starting 1¼ in. (3cm), from start of neck shaping and the other two spaced evenly between that and one already worked in rib.

Work 5 sts, join a second ball of yarn and work to end. Working both sides at the same time, work a further 3 rows, then work across all sts on foll row.

NECKBAND

With RS facing, using larger needles, starting at right center front, leave first 3 sts on hold, pick up and k6 sts from holder at center front, k36 (36:38:38:38) sts up front neck edge, k2 sts down right back neck edge, k19 (19:21:21:21) sts from holder at center back, k2 sts up left back neck edge, k36 (36:38:38:38) sts down left front neck, and k6 sts from holder at center front, leave rem 3 sts on hold. 107 (107:113:113:113) sts. Then starting with a RS row (so RS shows when turned back), work in knot pattern for 22 rows, centering the patt as follows:

XS and S

Row 7: K1, (p3tog, k3tog, p3tog) into next 3 sts, *k9, (p3tog, k3tog, p3tog) into next 3 sts; rep from * to last 7 sts, k7.

Row 15: K7, *(p3tog, k3tog, p3tog) into next 3 sts, k9; rep from * to last 4 sts, (p3tog, k3tog, p3tog) into next 3 sts, k1.

M, L and XL

Row 7: K1, *k9, (p3tog, k3tog, p3tog) into next 3 sts; rep from * to last 4 sts, k4.

Row 15: K4, *(p3tog, k3tog, p3tog) into next 3 sts, k9; rep from * to last st, k1.

At the same time work as follows:

Row 1: Slip 1, work to last 3 sts, yf, slip 1 purlwise, yb, turn.

Row 2: Slip 1 purlwise, work to last 3 sts, yb, slip 1 purlwise, yf, turn.

Row 3: Slip 1 purlwise, yb, work to last 5 sts, yf, slip 1 purlwise, yb, turn.

Row 4: Slip 1 purlwise, work to last 5 sts, yf, slip 1 purlwise, yb, turn.

Row 5: Slip 1 purlwise, yb, work to last 7 sts, yf, slip 1 purlwise, yb, turn.

Row 6: Slip 1 purlwise, work to last 7 sts, yf, slip 1 purlwise, yb, turn.

Work 22 rows turning as set, working 2 sts less between the turns on every 2 rows.

Next row: Slip 1 purlwise, yb, work to end of row. Change to smaller needles and work in 1 × 1 rib as follows:

Next row: Work in p1, k1, rib across all sts.

Next row: Work in rib across all sts, including 3 sts on hold.

Bind off loosely in rib over all 113 (113:119: 119:119) sts (including the 3 on hold at end of row). Set in sleeves, easing any fullness evenly across top of cap. Sew side and sleeve seams in one line. Work running st around each buttonhole to neaten. Attach 4 buttons on buttonband.

Marian

This timeless V-neck cardigan in easy garter stitch is a wardrobe staple. If you're not into stripes, just work the band, cuffs and pocket tops in a contrast color.

 Beginner

SIZES

	XS	S	M	L	XL	
To fit bust	32	34	36	38	40	in.
	81	86	91	97	102	cm

See diagram on page 91 for actual measurements.

YARN

14 (15:16:17:18) × 1¾ oz. (50g) balls of Debbie Bliss Cashmerino Chunky in Teal 10 (A)
2 (2:2:3:3) × 1¾ oz. (50g) balls of Debbie Bliss Cashmerino Chunky in Aubergine 08 (B)

NEEDLES

Pair each of US 10 (6mm) and US 10½ (7mm) needles
US 10 (6mm) circular needle
Stitch holders and markers

NOTIONS

5 buttons

GAUGE

13 sts and 26 rows to 4 in. (10cm) measured over garter st using US 10½ (7mm) needles. Change needle size if necessary to obtain this gauge.

ABBREVIATIONS

See page 12.

STITCHES

Garter stitch

Back

Using smaller needles and B, cast on
56 (60:64:66:70) sts and working in garter st throughout, work 1¼ in. (3cm), ending on a WS row. Change to larger needles and cont in A, dec 1 st at both ends of next row. 54 (58:62:64:68) sts. When work measures 5½ (5½:5½:5¾:5¾) in. [14 (14:14:14.5:14.5)cm] from cast-on edge ending on WS row, cont as follows:
Work 4 rows in B.
Work 8 rows in A.
Repeat these 12 rows twice more and then work 4 more rows in B (40 rows).
Cont in A to end, until work measures
20 (20:19½:20:20) in. [50 (50:49.5:50:50)cm] from cast-on edge, ending on a WS row.

SHAPE ARMHOLE

Bind off 3 (3:3:4:4) sts at beg of next 2 rows. Then dec 1 st at both ends of next and every foll alt row 3 (3:5:4:5) times in all. 42 (46:46:48:50) sts.
Cont as set until work measures 27½ (27½:27½: 28½:28½) in. [70 (70:70:72.25:72.25)cm] from cast-on edge, ending on a WS row.

SHAPE SHOULDER AND NECK

Next row (RS): Work 15 (17:16:17:17) sts, place center 12 (12:14:14:16) sts on holder, join a second ball of yarn and work to end. Working both sides at the same time, dec 1 st at both neck edges on next and foll alt row.

At the same time work and place 4 (5:4:5:5) sts on holder at armhole edge on next row, (for left back neck it will be foll row), and 4 (5:5:5:5) sts on foll alternate row. Bind off over all 13 (15:14:15:15) sts.

Left Front

POCKET LININGS (MAKE 2)
Using larger needles and A, cast on 16 sts and work 6 in. (15cm) in st st and then leave on holder.

Using smaller needles and B cast on 33 (35:37:38:40) sts and working in garter st throughout, work 1¼ in. (3cm), ending on a WS row. Change to larger needles and cont in A, dec 1 st at beg of next row. 32 (34:36:37:39) sts. When work measures 5½ (5½:5½:5¾:5¾) in. [14 (14:14:14.5:14.5)cm] from cast-on edge

ending on a WS row, cont as follows:
Work 4 rows in B.
Work 8 rows in A.
Repeat these 12 rows twice more and then work 4 more rows in B (40 rows).
Continue in A to end.
At the same time when work measures 7¼ in. (18.5cm) from cast-on edge, ending on a WS row, work pocket.

WORK POCKET
Work 7 (7:8:9:10) sts, place foll 16 sts on holder and work 16 sts in garter st in A from pocket lining, work rem 9 (11:12:12:13) sts.
Cont until work measures 18 (18:18:19:19) in. [45.75 (45.75:45.75:48.25:48.25)cm] from cast-on edge, ending on a RS row.

SHAPE NECKLINE

Dec 1 st at neck edge on next and every foll
3rd row 0 (0:0:0:4) times, then every foll 4th row
8 (8:13:13:10) times, then every foll 5th row
4 (4:0:0:0) times. 13 (15:14:15:15) sts.
At the same time when work measures
20 (20:19½:20:20) in. [50 (50:49.5:50:50)cm] from
cast-on edge, ending on a WS row, shape armhole.

SHAPE ARMHOLE

Bind off 3 (3:3:4:4) sts at beg of next row.
Work 1 row. Then dec 1 st at beg of next and
every foll alt row 3 (3:5:4:5) times in all.
Cont as set until work measures
27½ (27½:27½:28½:28½) in.
[70 (70:70:72.25:72.25)cm] from cast-on edge,
ending on a WS row.

SHAPE SHOULDER

Work and place 4 (5:4:5:5) sts on holder at
armhole edge. Work 1 row.
Work and place 4 (5:5:5:5) sts on holder at
armhole edge. Work 1 row.
Bind off over all 13 (15:14:15:15) sts.

Right Front

Mark position of 5 buttons on left front: first one
1¼ in. (3cm) from bottom, fifth one at bottom of
v-neck and other three spaced evenly between.
Work as for Left Front, reversing all shapings and
pocket placement, inserting buttonholes to
correspond to markers on RS rows as follows:
Work 2 sts, bind off 3 sts, work to end. Cast on
these sts when you come to them on foll row.

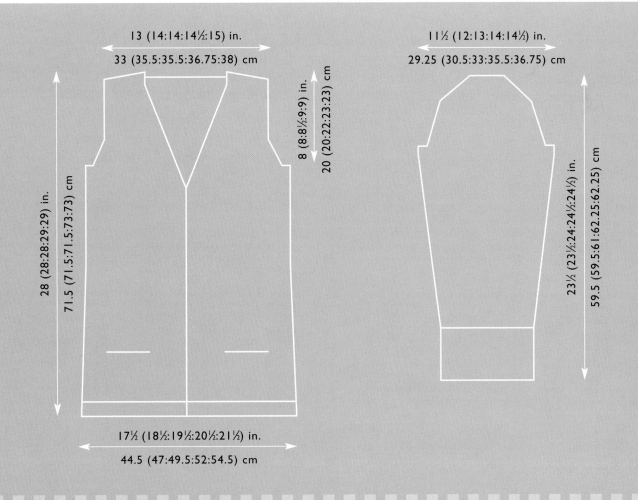

13 (14:14:14½:15) in.
33 (35.5:35.5:36.75:38) cm

8 (8:8½:9:9) in.
20 (20:22:23:23) cm

28 (28:28:29:29) in.
71.5 (71.5:71.5:73:73) cm

17½ (18½:19½:20½:21½) in.
44.5 (47:49.5:52:54.5) cm

11½ (12:13:14:14½) in.
29.25 (30.5:33:35.5:36.75) cm

23½ (23½:24:24½:24½) in.
59.5 (59.5:61:62.25:62.25) cm

Sleeves

Using larger needles and B cast on
30 (30:30:32:32) sts and working in garter st
throughout, work 26 rows as follows:
Work 6 rows in B.
Work 4 rows in A.
Work 6 rows in B.
Work 4 rows in A.
Work 6 rows in B.
Change to smaller needles and transfer knitting to
one of these, break yarn and start at other side (so
that when cuff is turned back the right side will be
on the outside). With WS facing, work a further
26 rows as above. Then change to larger needles
and continue in A to end, inc as follows:
XS 1 st at both ends of every 19th row twice, then
every 20th row twice. 38 sts.
S 1 st at both ends of every 15th row twice, then
every 16th row 3 times. 40 sts.
M 1 st at both ends of every 13th row twice,
then every 14th row 4 times. 42 sts.
L 1 st at both ends of every 11th row twice,
then every 12th row 5 times. 46 sts.
XL 1 st at both ends of every 10th row 6 times,
then every 11th row twice. 48 sts.
Cont as set until work measures
22 (22:22½:22½:22½) in. [56 (56:57:57:57)cm]
from cast-on edge.

SHAPE SLEEVE CAP

Bind off 3 (3:3:4:4) sts at beg of next 2 rows.
Then dec as follows:
XS 1 st at both ends of next and every 4th row
twice, then every 5th row 4 times. 18 sts.
S 1 st at both ends of next and every 4th row
7 times. 18 sts.
M 1 st at both ends of next and every 3rd row
4 times, then every 4th row 4 times. 18 sts.
L 1 st at both ends of next and every 3rd row
once, then every 4th row 7 times. 20 sts.

XL 1 st at both ends of next and every 3rd row
5 times, then every 4th row 4 times. 20 sts.
Bind off 2 sts at beg of next 4 rows. Bind off rem
10 (10:10:12:12) sts.

Finishing

POCKETS

Using smaller needles and color to keep striped
pattern correct, pick up 16 sts from holder at top
of pocket. Work 2 rows in garter st, keeping color
sequence correct, then bind off.
Join shoulder seams.
Set in sleeves placing any fullness evenly over top
of sleeve cap. Join side and sleeve seams in one
line. Turn sleeves back on RS and catch in place
along vertical seam on inside, leaving cast-on edge
open. Using an invisible slip stitch, sew pocket
linings in place to sit on top of welt.

BAND

Using circular needle and A, but working back and
forth, with RS facing and starting at bottom right
front edge, pick up and k96 (96:96:100:100) sts
evenly to shoulder seam, k2 sts down back neck
edge, k12 (12:14:14:16) sts from holder at center
back, k2 sts up other side back neck edge and
k96 (96:96:100:100) sts evenly down to bottom
Left Front. 208 (208:210:218:220) sts.
Knit 1 row and then bind off knitwise.
Attach 5 buttons on left front opposite buttonholes.

Tiffany

Turn heads wearing this classic bouclé jacket in fiery red with three-quarter sleeves. When I look at this sweater I think of Audrey Hepburn.

 ## Beginner

SIZES

	XS	S	M	L	XL	
To fit bust	32	34	36	38	40	in.
	81	86	91	97	102	cm

See diagram on page 97 for actual measurements.

YARN
9 (9:10:10:11) × 1¾ oz. (50g) balls of Debbie Bliss Cashmerino Astrakhan in Scarlet 14

NEEDLES
Pair of US 6 (4mm) needles
US 6 (4mm) circular needle
Stitch holders

NOTIONS
3 buttons

GAUGE
16 sts and 28 rows to 4 in. (10cm) measured over garter stitch. Change needle size if necessary to obtain this gauge.

ABBREVIATIONS
See page 12.

STITCHES
Garter stitch

Back

Using straight needles, cast on 66 (70:74:78:82) sts and working in garter st throughout, knit 2 rows, then dec as follows: Dec 1 st at both ends of next and every foll 10th row 4 times in all. 58 (62:66:70:74) sts. Work 1 in. (2.5cm) without shaping, then inc 1 st at both ends of next and every foll 12th row 4 times in all. 66 (70:74:78:82) sts. Cont as set until work measures 11½ (11½:11½:11:11½) in. [29.25 (29.25:29.25: 28:29.25)cm] from cast-on edge, ending on a WS row.

SHAPE ARMHOLE
Bind off 3 (3:3:4:4) sts at beg of next 2 rows. Then dec 1 st at both ends of next and every foll alt row 4 (4:6:6:7) times in all. 52 (56:56:58:60) sts. Cont as set until work measures 18½ (18½:18½:19½:19½) in. [47 (47:47:49.5:49.5)cm] from cast-on edge, ending on a WS row.

WRAPPING A STITCH

With yarn in back, slip the next st as if to purl. Bring yarn to front of work and slip stitch back to left needle. Turn the work.

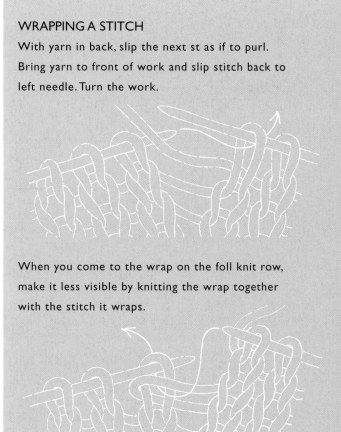

When you come to the wrap on the foll knit row, make it less visible by knitting the wrap together with the stitch it wraps.

SHAPE SHOULDER AND NECK

Next row (RS): Work 16 (17:17:17:18) sts, place center 20 (22:22:24:24) sts on holder, join a second ball of yarn and work to end. Working both sides at the same time, dec 1 st at both neck edges on next and foll alt row.

At the same time work and place 4 (5:5:5:5) sts on holder at armhole edge on next row, (for left back neck it will be foll row), and 5 sts on foll alt row. Bind off over all 14 (15:15:15:16) sts.

Left Front

Using straight needles, cast on 40 (42:44:46:49) sts and working in garter stitch throughout, knit 2 rows, then dec as follows:

Dec 1 st at beg of next and every foll 10th row 4 times in all. 36 (38:40:42:45) sts.

Work 1 in. (2.5cm) without shaping, then inc 1 st at both ends of next and every foll 12th row 4 times in all. 40 (42:44:46:49) sts

Cont as set until work measures 11½ (11½:11½: 11:11½) in. [29.25 (29.25:29.25:28:29.25)cm] from cast-on edge, ending on a WS row.

SHAPE ARMHOLE

Bind off 3 (3:3:4:4) sts at beg of next row. Work 1 row. Then dec 1 st at armhole edge of next and every foll alt row 4 (4:6:6:7) times in all. 33 (35:35:36:38) sts.

Cont as set until work measures 16½ (16½:16½: 17½:17½) in. [42 (42:42:44.5:44.5)cm] from cast-on edge, ending on a RS row.

SHAPE NECK

Work and place 8 (8:8:9:9) sts at beg of next row on holder, then wrap and place 1 st on hold at neck edge on next and every foll alt row 6 (5:5:5:4) times, then every row 5 (7:7:7:9) times, (no wraps on every row).

At the same time when work measures 18½ (18½: 18½:19½:19½) in. [47 (47:47:49.5:49.5)cm] from cast-on edge, ending on a WS row, shape shoulder.

SHAPE SHOULDER

Start on Row 15 of neck shaping.

Work and place 4 (5:5:5:5) sts on holder at armhole edge, work to end of row. Work 1 row. Work and place 5 sts on holder at armhole edge, work to end of row. Work 1 row. Bind off over all 14 (15:15:15:16) sts.

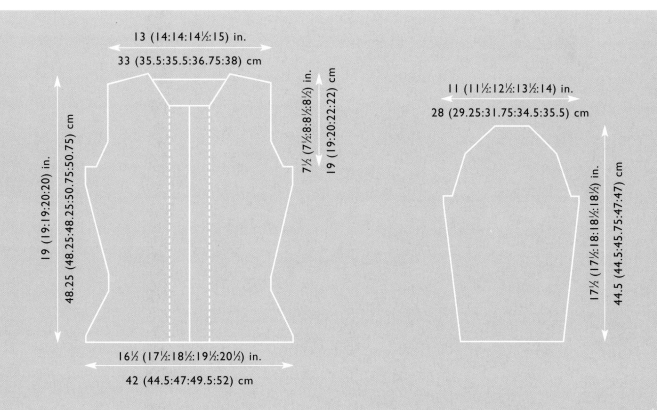

13 (14:14:14½:15) in.
33 (35.5:35.5:36.75:38) cm

7½ (7½:8:8½:8½) in.
19 (19:20:22:22) cm

19 (19:19:20:20) in.
48.25 (48.25:48.25:50.75:50.75) cm

16½ (17½:18½:19½:20½) in.
42 (44.5:47:49.5:52) cm

11 (11½:12½:13½:14) in.
28 (29.25:31.75:34.5:35.5) cm

17½ (17½:18:18½:18½) in.
44.5 (44.5:45.75:47:47) cm

Right Front

Mark position of 3 buttons on Left Front, first one 1 in. (2.5cm) down from neck edge, third 5½ (5½:5½:6:6) in. [14 (14:14:15.25:15.25)cm] up from bottom and second spaced evenly between. Work as for Left Front, reversing all shapings and inserting buttonholes opposite markers on RS rows to correspond to markers on Left Front as follows:

Next row: Work 2 sts, bind off 5 sts, work to end of row.

Next row: Work to last 7 sts, cast on 5 sts, work 2 sts.

Work in back of 5 cast on sts on next row.

Sleeves

Using straight needles, cast on 38 (38:38:40:40) sts and working in garter stitch throughout, knit 14 rows, then inc 1 st at both ends of next and then every 30th (20th:13th:11th:9th) row 3 (4:6:7:8) times in all. 44 (46:50:54:56) sts.
Cont as set until work measures 12 (12:12½:12½:12½) in. [30.5 (30.5:31.75:31.75:31.75)cm] from cast-on edge, ending on a WS row.

SHAPE SLEEVE CAP

Bind off 3 (3:3:4:4) sts at beg of next 2 rows. Then dec 1 st at both ends of every foll 4th row 7 (4:0:2:0) times, then every 3rd row 2 (6:10:10:12) times, then every 2nd row 0 (0:2:0:1) times. 20 (20:20:22:22) sts.
Bind off 2 sts at beg of next 4 rows. Bind off rem 12 (12:12:14:14) sts

Finishing

Join shoulder seams.
Set in sleeves placing any fullness evenly over top of sleeve cap. Join side and sleeve seams in one line.

COLLAR

Using circular needle, but working back and forth, with RS facing, starting at right front neck edge, pick up and k8 (8:8:9:9) sts from holder at center front, k17 sts from holders up to shoulder (when st is wrapped, knit first into wrap below and then into st above), k3 sts down right back neck edge, k20 (22:22:24:24) sts from holder at center back, k3 sts up left back neck edge, k17 sts from holders up to shoulder (knit first into wrap below and then into st above) and k8 (8:8:9:9) sts from holder at left front neck edge. 76 (78:78:82:82) sts. Work 1 in. (2.5cm) in garter stitch, then leave sts on hold.

BANDS

Using circular needle, but working back and forth, with RS facing, starting at bottom right front, pick up and k76 (76:76:80:80) sts up center front, k76 (78:78:82:82) sts from holder around neckline and k76 (76:76:80:80) sts down left center front. 228 (230:230:242:242) sts.
Bind off loosely. Attach 3 buttons opposite buttonholes.

Susy

This ubiquitous black turtle neck has beads for added sparkle.
This sweater offers a chance to learn to knit with beads, or you
can knit the classic version without beads for a more casual look.

 Intermediate

SIZES

	XS	S	M	L	XL	
To fit bust	32	34	36	38	42	in.
	81	86	91	97	102	cm

See diagram on page 102 for actual measurements.

YARN
9 (10:11:11:12) × 1¾ oz. (50g) balls of Debbie Bliss Cathay in Black 01

NEEDLES
Pair each of US 3 (3.25mm) and US 5 (3.75mm) needles
US 3 (3.25mm) and US 5 (3.75mm) circular needles
Stitch holders

NOTIONS
Approximately 604 (638:668:694:718) small black glass beads

GAUGE
22 sts and 30 rows to 4 in. (10cm) measured over stockinette stitch using US 5 (3.75mm) needles. Change needle size if necessary to obtain this gauge.

ABBREVIATIONS
See page 12.

STITCHES
Seed stitch (odd no sts)
Stockinette stitch

Back

Thread approx 172 (184:192:204:216) beads onto ball of yarn. Using smaller needles cast on 89 (95:99:105:111) sts and work 8 rows in seed st, placing beads on RS rows only on 3rd and subsequently every alt stitch across row (beads are placed on every knit st, except at side edges, do not place in seam). Change to larger needles and cont in st st to end, dec as follows:

XS and S 1 st at both ends of every 5th row 5 times. 79 (85) sts.

M, L and XL 1 st at both ends of every 7th row twice, then every 8th row twice. 91 (97:103) sts. Work a further 10 rows, then inc as follows:

XS and S 1 st at both ends of every 6th row 5 times. 89 (95) sts.

M, and XL 1 st at both ends of every 6th row twice, then every 7th row twice. 99 (111) sts.

L 1 st at both ends of every 5th row twice, then every 6th row twice. 105 sts.

Cont as set until work measures 11½ (11½:11½:11:11½) in. [29.25 (29.25:29.25:28:29.25)cm] from cast-on edge ending on a WS row.

SHAPE ARMHOLE
Bind off 5 (5:6:6:6) sts at beg of next 2 rows, then dec 1 st at both ends of next and every alt row 4 (4:5:7:9) times. 71 (77:77:79:81) sts. Cont as set until work measures 18½ (18½:19:19:19½) in. [47 (47:48.25:48.25:49.5)cm] from cast-on edge, ending on a WS row.

SHAPE SHOULDER AND NECK

Next row (RS): Work 21 (23:23:23:24) sts, place center 29 (31:31:33:33) sts on holder, join a second ball of yarn and work to end. Working both sides at the same time, dec 1 st at both neck edges on next and foll alt row.

At the same time work and place 6 (7:7:7:7) sts on holder at armhole edge on next row (for left back neck it will be foll row), and 6 (7:7:7:7) sts on foll alt row. Bind off over all 19 (21:21:21:22) sts.

Front

Work as for Back until work measures 16½ (16½:17:17:17½) in. [42 (42:43:43:44.5)cm] from cast-on edge, ending on a WS row.

SHAPE NECKLINE

Next row (RS): Work 27 (30:30:30:31) sts, place center 17 (17:17:19:19) sts on holder, join a second ball of yarn and work to end. Working both sides at the same time, dec 1 st at both neck edges on next and every row 4 (5:5:5:5) times, then every alt row 4 times. 19 (21:21:21:22) sts. Cont until work measures 18½ (18½:19:19:19½) in. [47 (47:48.25:48.25:49.5)cm] from cast-on edge, ending on a WS row (RS row for right neck edge).

SHAPE SHOULDER

Work and place 6 (7:7:7:7) sts on holder at armhole edge, work to end of row. Work 1 row. Work and place 6 (7:7:7:7) sts on holder at armhole edge, work to end of row. Work 1 row. Bind off over all 19 (21:21:21:22) sts.

Sleeves

Thread approx 88 (88:96:96:96) beads onto ball of yarn. Using smaller needles cast on 45 (45:49:49:49) sts and work 8 rows in seed st, placing beads on RS rows only on 3rd and subsequently every alt stitch across row (every knit st as before). Change to larger needles and cont in st st to end, inc as follows:

XS 1 st at both ends of every foll 14th row 8 times. 61 sts.

S 1 st at both ends of every foll 12th row 5 times, then every 13th row 4 times. 63 sts.

M 1 st at both ends of every foll 11th row 4 times, then every 12th row 6 times. 69 sts.

L 1 st at both ends of every foll 8th row once, then every 9th row 12 times. 75 sts.

XL 1 st at both ends of every foll 8th row 10 times, then every 9th row 4 times. 77 sts.

Cont until work measures 18 (18:18½:18½:18½) in. [45.75 (45.75:47:47:47)cm] from cast-on edge, ending on a WS row.

ATTACHING BEADS

On a RS row: Work to position of beaded stitch. Bring the yarn forward to front of work and push a bead down the yarn so that it lies against the needle at the front of the work. Slip the next stitch purlwise, leaving the bead in front of the slipped stitch. Take the yarn to the back and cont to work as normal.

On a WS row: Work to the position of the bead, take the yarn to the back of the work and place the bead so that it lies on RS of work against the needle. Slip the next stitch purlwise, leaving the bead behind the slipped stitch. Take the yarn to the front and cont to purl as set.

SHAPE SLEEVE CAP

Bind off 5 (5:6:6:6) sts at beg of next 2 rows.
Then dec 1 st at both ends of next, then every foll
alt row 0 (1:10:9:12) times, then every 3rd row
9 (11:5:7:5) times, then every 4th row
2 (0:0:0:0) times. 27 (27:27:29:29) sts.
Bind off 3 sts at beg of next 4 rows. Bind off rem
15 (15:15:17:17) sts.

Finishing

Set in sleeves.
Sew side and sleeve seams in one line.

COLLAR

Thread approx 84 (86:90:94:94) beads onto ball of
yarn. Using smaller circular needle, with RS
facing, starting at left shoulder seam, pick up
and k17 (17:19:19:19) sts down right neck edge
17 (17:17:19:19) sts from holder at center front,
k17 (17:19:19:19) sts up left neck edge, k2 sts
down left back neck edge, 29 (31:31:33:33) sts
from holder at center back and k2 sts up right back
neck edge. 84 (86:90:94:94) sts. Join into the
round and work 7.5cm (3 in.) in patt as follows:
Round 1: *P1, k1, p1, k1, p2, k1, p1; rep from *
around.
Round 2: *(P1, k1); rep from * around.
Rep these 2 rounds.
Then change to larger circular needle and work a
further 4 in. (10cm) in patt placing bead on 1st
and every alt st on two final Round 2s.

NOTE

Place beads on WS so that when collar is turned
down the beads are on RS.
Bind off in pattern.

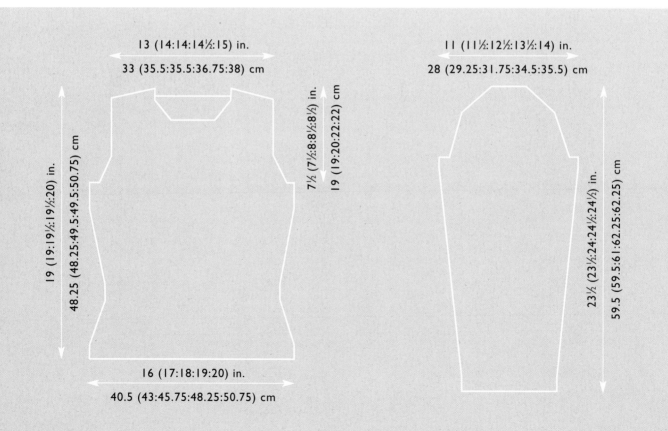

13 (14:14:14½:15) in.
33 (35.5:35.5:36.75:38) cm

7½ (7½:8:8½:8½) in.
19 (19:20:22:22) cm

19 (19:19½:19½:20) in.
48.25 (48.25:49.5:49.5:50.75) cm

16 (17:18:19:20) in.
40.5 (43:45.75:48.25:50.75) cm

11 (11½:12½:13½:14) in.
28 (29.25:31.75:34.5:35.5) cm

23½ (23½:24:24½:24½) in.
59.5 (59.5:61:62.25:62.25) cm

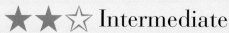

Maria

A must-have in any summer wardrobe, this delicate camisole is the perfect project for improving lace knitters, because there's no shaping in the snowflake pattern.

★ ★ ☆ Intermediate

SIZES

	XS	S	M	L	XL	
To fit bust	32	34	36	40	44	in.
	81	86	91	102	112	cm

See diagram below for actual measurements. The measurements above are larger than those on the diagram as the garment is designed to cling.

YARN

2 (2:3:3:3) × 1 oz. (25g) balls of Rowan Kidsilk Haze in Grace 580

NEEDLES

Pair each of US 6 (4mm) and US 7 (4.5mm) needles
US 6 (4mm) circular needle
Stitch holders

GAUGE

20 sts and 24 rows to 4 in. (10cm) measured over pattern using US 7 (4.5mm) needles, after blocking. Change needle size if necessary to obtain this gauge.

ABBREVIATIONS

See page 12.

STITCHES

Garter stich

Stockinette stitch

Snowflake eyelet pattern (multiple of 8 + 5)

  Row 1 (WS and all other WS rows): Purl.

  Row 2: K4, *ssk, yo, k1, yo, k2tog, k3; rep from *. End last repeat k1.

  Row 4: K5, *yo, slip 2-k1-p2sso, yo, k5, repeat from *.

  Row 6: As Row 2.

  Row 8: Ssk, yo, k1, yo, k2tog, *k3, ssk, yo, k1, yo, k2tog; rep from *.

  Row 10: K1, *yo, slip 2-k1-p2sso, yo, k5, rep from *. End last repeat k1.

  Row 12: As Row 8.

  Repeat Rows 1–12.

Picot point bind-off – Bind off 2 sts, *slip rem st on RH needle onto LH needle, cast on 2 sts, bind off 4 sts; rep from * to end and fasten off rem st.

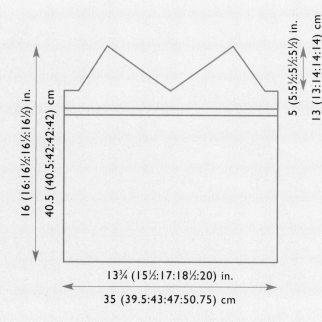

16 (16:16½:16½:16½) in.
40.5 (40.5:42:42:42) cm

13¾ (15½:17:18½:20) in.
35 (39.5:43:47:50.75) cm

5 (5:5½:5½:5½) in.
13 (13:14:14:14) cm

Back

Using smaller needles cast on
69 (77:85:93:101) sts and work 4 rows in garter st.
Change to larger needes and cont in Snowflake
Eyelet Pattern until work measures 9 in
(22.75cm), ending on a WS row. Work 6 rows in
garter st and then leave on holder.
At the same time on Row 3 work eyelets as follows:
XS K2, *k2tog, yo, k1; rep from * to last st, k1.
S K2, *k2tog, yo, k1; rep from * to end.
M K1, *k2tog, yo, k1; rep from * to end.
L K2, *k2tog, yo, k1; rep from * to last st, k1.
XL K2, *k2tog, yo, k1; rep from * to end.
Cont in st st until work measures 11 in. (28cm).
Bind off.

Front

Work as for Back up to but not including bind off,
then cont in st st to end.

SHAPE ARMHOLES

Work and place 5 sts on holder on next 2 rows.
Then dec as follows:
XS 1 st at both ends of next, then every 5th row
once, then every 4th row 6 times. 53 sts.
S 1 st at both ends of next, then every 3rd row
7 times, then every alt row 4 times. 53 sts.
M 1 st at both ends of next, then every 3rd row
5 times, then every alt row 8 times. 57 sts.
L 1 st at both ends of next, then every alt
16 times, then every row once. 57 sts.
XL 1 st at both ends of next, then every alt
14 times, then every row 5 times. 61 sts.
At the same time when work measures 11½ in.
(29.25cm) from cast-on edge, ending on a WS row,
shape neckline.

SHAPE NECKLINE

You should start on Row 5 of armhole shaping.
Next row (RS): Work to center st, place center st
on holder, join a second ball of yarn and work to
end. Working both sides at the same time and
continuing with armhole shaping, dec 1 st at
both neck edges on next and every foll alt row
6 (6:6:8:6) times, then every row
14 (14:16:14:18) times. Leave last st on holder.

Finishing

Join side seams.
With RS of front facing and using smaller needles,
start with stitch at top of left cup and pick up and
k24 (24:26:26:26) sts down to center st.
K1 st from holder at center front and
k24 (24:26:26:26) sts up to and including st
at top of right cup.
49 (49:53:53:53) sts. Knit 1 row and then bind off
using picot point bind-off (see page 104). Then
using circular US 6 (4mm) needle and with RS
facing, cast on 52 sts (lengthen or shorten straps
here). Pick up and knit 26 (26:28:28:28) sts down
side of right cup, 5 sts from holder at armhole
edge, 69 (77:85:93:101) sts across back, 5 sts
from holder at other front armhole edge,
26 (26:28:28:28) sts up side of left cup and then
cast on a further 52 sts (again lengthen or shorten
here) for other strap. 235 (243:255:263:271) sts.
Knit 1 row and then bind off using picot point
bind-off.
Attach straps to back in line with fronts. Thread
ribbon through eyelets, and tie.

Rima

*Classy, simple lines make this plunge-neck sweater an easy knit.
To dress it up for the evening, trim the hem, cuffs, and collar
with a couple of rows of Lurex.*

 Beginner

SIZES

	XS	S	M	L	XL	
To fit bust	32	34	36	38	40	in.
	81	86	91	97	102	cm

See diagram on page 110 for actual measurements.

YARN
8 (9:10:10:11) × 1¾ oz. (50g) balls of Artesano Inca Cloud Alpaca in Fuchsia 57

NEEDLES
Pair of each US 3 (3.25mm) and US 5 (3.75mm) needles
US 3 (3.25mm), US 5 (3.75mm) and US 6 (4mm) circular needles
Stitch holders

GAUGE
24 sts and 32 rows to 4 in. (10cm) measured over stockinette stitch using US 5 (3.75mm) needles. Change needle size if necessary to obtain this gauge.

ABBREVIATIONS
See page 12.

STITCHES
1 × 1 rib
Stockinette stitch

Back

Using smaller needles, cast on
97 (103:109:115:121) sts and work in 1 × 1 rib for
4 in. (10cm). Change to larger needles and work in
st st to end. Cont until work measures
11½ (11½:11½:11:11½) in.
[29.25 (29.25:29.25:28:29.25)cm] from cast-on
edge, ending on a WS row.

SHAPE ARMHOLE
Bind off 5 (5:6:6:6) sts at beg of next 2 rows, then
dec 1 st at both ends of next and every alt row
4 (4:6:8:9) times. 79 (85:85:87:91) sts.
Cont as set until work measures
18½ (18½:19:19:19½) in.
[47 (47:48.25:48.25:49.5)cm] from cast-on edge,
ending on a WS row.

SHAPE SHOULDER AND NECK
Next row (RS): Work 27 (30:28:29:31) sts, place
center 25 (25:29:29:29) sts on holder, join a
second ball of yarn and work to end. Working both
sides at the same time, dec 1 st at both neck edges
on next and foll alt row.
At the same time, work and place 8 (9:8:9:9) sts on
holder at armhole edge on next row (for left back
neck it will be foll row), and 8 (9:9:9:10) sts on foll
alt row. Bind off over all 25 (28:26:27:29) sts.

Front

Work as for Back until work measures
8 (8:8½:8½:9) in. [20.5 (20.5:21.5:21.5:22.75)cm]
ending on a WS row.

SHAPE NECKLINE
Next row (RS): Work 48 (51:54:57:60) sts, place
center st on holder, join a second ball of yarn and
work to end. Dec 1 st at neck edge on next, then
every foll 5th row 2 (2:14:14:14) times, then every
foll 6th row 11 (11:1:1:1) times.
14 (14:16:16:16) sts decreased.
At the same time when work measures 11½
(11½:11½:11:11½) in. [29.25 (29.25:29.25:
28:29.25)cm] from cast-on edge ending on a WS
row (RS row for right neck edge), shape armhole.

SHAPE ARMHOLE
Bind off 5 (5:6:6:6) sts at beg of next row. Then
dec 1 st at armhole edge of next and every alt row
4 (4:6:8:9) times.

Cont until work measures
18½ (18½:19:19:19½) in. [47 (47:48.25:48.25:
49.5)cm] from cast-on edge, ending on a WS row
(RS row for right neck edge).

SHAPE SHOULDER
Work and place 8 (9:8:9:9) sts on holder at
armhole edge, work to end of row.
Work 1 row. Work and place 8 (9:9:9:10) sts on
holder at armhole edge, work to end of row. Work
1 row. Bind off over all 25 (28:26:27:29) sts.

Sleeves

Using smaller needles cast on 52 (52:54:54:54) sts
and work in 1 × 1 rib for 4 in. (10cm). Change to
larger needles and cont in st st to end, inc as
follows:
XS 1 st at both ends of every foll 13th row twice,
then every 14th row 5 times. 66 sts.
S 1 st at both ends of every foll 10th row 3 times,
then every 11th row 6 times. 70 sts.

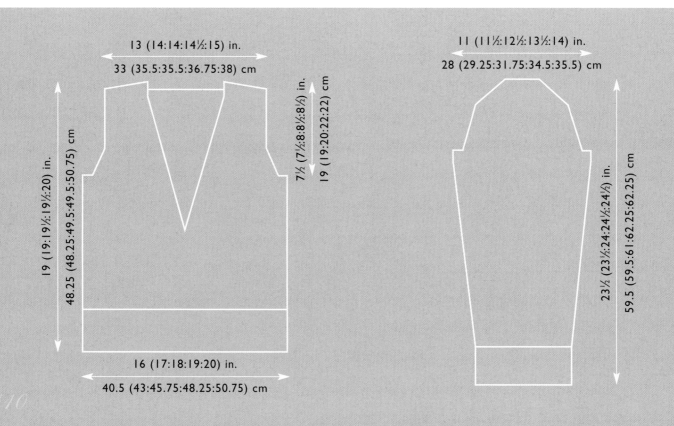

13 (14:14:14½:15) in.
33 (35.5:35.5:36.75:38) cm
7½ (7½:8:8½:8½) in.
19 (19:20:22:22) cm
19 (19:19½:19½:20) in.
48.25 (48.25:49.5:49.5:50.75) cm
16 (17:18:19:20) in.
40.5 (43:45.75:48.25:50.75) cm

11 (11½:12½:13½:14) in.
28 (29.25:31.75:34.5:35.5) cm
23½ (23½:24:24½:24½) in.
59.5 (59.5:61:62.25:62.25) cm

M 1 st at both ends of every foll 9th row 10 times, then every 10th row once. 76 sts.

L 1 st at both ends of every foll 7th row 12 times, then every 8th row twice. 82 sts.

XL 1 st at both ends of every foll 6th row 5 times, then every 7th row 10 times. 84 sts.

Cont until work measures
18 (18:18½:18½:18½) in.
[45.75 (45.75:47:47:47)cm] from cast-on edge, ending on a WS row.

SHAPE SLEEVE CAP

Bind off 5 (5:6:6:6) sts at beg of next 2 rows. Then dec 1 st at both ends of next row and then every 3rd row 10 (6:4:2:0) times, then every alt row 4 (10:13:18:21) times. 26 (26:28:28:28) sts. Bind off 3 sts at beg of next 4 rows. Bind off rem 14 (14:16:16:16) sts.

Finishing

Set in sleeves.
Sew side and sleeve seams in one line.

NECKBAND

With RS facing and using US 3 (3.25mm) circular needle, starting at left shoulder seam, pick up and k88 sts down left front neck edge, k1 st from holder at center front, k88 sts up right neck edge, 2 sts down right back neck edge, 25 (25:29:29:29) sts from holder at center back and 2 sts up left back neck edge. 206 (206:210:210:210) sts. Join into the round and work 1 in. (2.5cm) in 1 × 1 rib, then 2 in. (5cm) in 1 × 1 rib on US 5 (3.75mm) circular needle, then 3 in. (7.5cm) in 1 × 1 rib, on US 6 (4mm) circular needle as follows:
Round 1: *K1, p1; rep from * around.
Rep Round 1.
Bind off loosely in rib.

Ondine

Get yourself in party mood with this chic wrap. Knitted mainly in reversible garter stitch, it has a pretty lace edging. If you're feeling creative, add a favorite edging of your own.

★☆☆ Beginner

SIZES
One size – approximately 20 × 66 in. (51 × 168cm)

YARN
9 × 1¾ oz. (50g) balls of Debbie Bliss Baby Cashmerino in Mint 003

NEEDLES
US 6 (4mm) needles
Markers

GAUGE
21 sts and 28 rows to 4 in. (10cm) measured over garter st when blocked. Change needle size if necessary to obtain this gauge.
Note: before blocking the piece will be smaller than required size, therefore block your swatch before measuring.

ABBREVIATIONS
See page 12.

STITCHES
Garter stitch

Lace edging – Multiple of 23 sts.
 Foundation row: Knit.
 Row 1 (RS): Slip 1, k2, *yo, k2tog; rep from * to end.
 Row 2: K17, p1, k1, p1, k3.
 Row 3: Slip 1, k2, [yo, k2tog] twice, k16.
 Row 4: K17, p1, k1, p1, k3.
 Rows 5 and 9: Slip1, k2, [yo, k2tog] twice, k16.
 Row 6: K1, *yo firmly 4 times, k1; rep from * to last 6 sts, p1, k1, p1, k3.
 Row 7: Slip 1, k2, [yo, k2tog] twice, *drop the 4 yo's, slip next st; rep from * to end – 16 long sts, then slip the 16 long sts back to LH needle, [slip sts 5–8 over sts 1–4 and back to LH needle, k8] twice.
 Rows 8 and 10: K17, p1, k1, p1, k3.
 Rep Rows 1–10, ending on Row 2.

Shawl

Cast on 105 sts and knit 1 row.
Row 1 (RS): K82 sts, place marker for start of lace edging, work row 1 of lace edging patt over rem 23 sts.
Row 2: Work row 2 of lace edging patt (23 sts), slip marker, k82 sts.
Cont as above through all 10 rows of lace edging pattern, working 82 sts of garter st (at beg on odd rows and at end on even rows) with 23 sts of lace edging at left edge.
Work the 10 rows as above 46 times, then work Rows 1 and 2. 462 rows.
Bind off.

66 in. (168cm)

20 in. (51cm)

Short or long, with hood or collar, the choice is yours with this gossamer knit. Wear it over a skimpy top on chilly evenings and you can be sure your fashion sense will not be compromised.

 Beginner

SIZES

	XS	S	M	L	XL	
To fit bust	32	34	36	38	40	in.
	81	86	91	97	102	cm

See diagram on page 116 for actual measurements.
Instructions for a shorter version are given within the pattern.

YARN
12 (12:13:13:14) × 1 oz. (25g) balls of Rowan Kidsilk Haze in Elegance 577 (longer version)
4 (4:5:5:6) × 1 oz. (25g) balls of Rowan Kidsilk Haze in Liqueur 595 (shorter version)

NEEDLES
Pair of US 7 (4.5mm) needles
US 7 (4.5mm) circular needle
Stitch holders

GAUGE
20 sts and 28 rows to 4 in. (10cm) measured over pattern.
Change needle size if necessary to obtain this gauge.

ABBREVIATIONS
See page 12.

STITCHES
Stockinette stitch
Stockinette stitch in the round

Back

Using straight needles cast on 90 (96:102:108:114) sts and starting with a knit row, work 8 rows in stocking st.

Next row (RS): K6, then rotate the LH needle counter-clockwise through 360 degrees (a whole circle), then k another 6 sts and rotate the LH needle again counter-clockwise through 360 degrees. Cont to k6 sts and rotate LH needle to end of row. Starting with a WS row, work in st st to end. Cont until work measures 20 (20:20½:20:21) in. [50.75 (50.75:52:50.75:53.5)cm], ending on a WS row.

SHAPE ARMHOLE
Note: for shorter version, change length here to 12 (12:12½:12:13) in. [30.5 (30.5:31.75:30.5:33)cm]. Dec 1 st at both ends of next and every foll alt row 6 (7:7:8:9) times in all. 78 (82:88:92:96) sts. Cont as set until work measures 27½ (27½:28½:28½:29½) in. [70 (70:72.25:72.25:75)cm], ending on a WS row. For shorter version cont until work measures 19½ (19½:20½:20½:21½) in. [49.5 (49.5:52:52:54.5)cm], ending on a WS row.

SHAPE SHOULDER AND NECK
Next row (RS): Work 16 (18:21:23:25) sts, place center 46 sts on holder, join a second ball of yarn and work to end. Working both sides at the same time, place 1 st on holder at both neck edges on next and foll alt row.

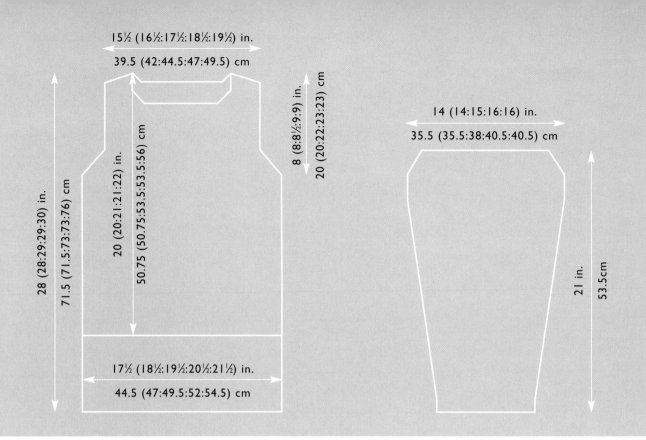

Dimensions (Body)

15½ (16½:17½:18½:19½) in.
39.5 (42:44.5:47:49.5) cm

8 (8:8½:9:9) in.
20 (20:22:23:23) cm

20 (20:21:21:22) in.
50.75 (50.75:53.5:53.5:56) cm

28 (28:29:29:30) in.
71.5 (71.5:73:73:76) cm

17½ (18½:19½:20½:21½) in.
44.5 (47:49.5:52:54.5) cm

Dimensions (Sleeve)

14 (14:15:16:16) in.
35.5 (35.5:38:40.5:40.5) cm

21 in.
53.5 cm

At the same time work and place 4 (5:6:7:7) sts on holder at armhole edge on next row, (for left back neck it will be foll row), and 5 (5:6:7:8) sts on foll alternate row. Bind off over all 14 (16:19:21:23) sts.

Front

Work as for Back until work measures 25½ (25½:26½:26½:26½:27½) in. [64.75 (64.75:67.25:67.25:70)cm], ending on a WS row. For shorter version cont until work measures 17½ (17½:18½:18½:19½) in. [44.5 (44.5:47:47:49.5)cm], ending on a WS row.

SHAPE NECK

Patt 26 (28:31:33:35) sts, place 26 sts on holder for neck and rem 26 (28:31:33:35) sts on another holder. Then work and place 1 st on holder at neck edge on next and every foll row 12 times. 14 (16:19:21:23) sts. Cont as set until work measures 27½ (27½:28½: 28½:29½) in. [70 (70:72.25:72.25:75)cm], ending on a WS row. For shorter version cont until work measures 19½ (19½:20½:20½:20½:21½) in. [49.5 (49.5:52:52:54.5)cm], ending on a WS row.

SHAPE SHOULDER

Work and place 4 (5:6:7:7) sts on holder at armhole edge. Work 1 row.
Work and place 5 (5:6:7:8) sts on holder at armhole edge. Work 1 row.
Bind off over whole 14 (16:19:21:23) sts.
Join second ball of yarn to other side and work in patt to end, reversing all shapings.

Sleeves

Cast on 42 (42:42:48:48) sts and starting with a knit row, work 8 rows in stocking st.
Next row (RS): K6, then rotate the LH needle counter-clockwise through 360 degrees (a whole circle), then k another 6 sts and rotate the LH needle again counter-clockwise through 360 degrees. Cont to k6 sts and rotate LH needle to end of row. Cont in st st to end, starting with a WS row, inc 1 st at both ends of every 7th row 0 (0:10:14:14) times, then every 8th row 8 (8:6:2:2) times, then every 9th row 6 (6:0:0:0) times. 70 (70:74:80:80) sts. Cont as set until work measures 19¼ (19:19:18¾:18½) in. [49 (48.25:48.25:47.5:47)cm].

SHAPE TOP OF SLEEVE

Dec 1 st at both ends of next and every foll alt row 6 (7:7:8:9) times in all. Bind off rem 58 (56:60:58:62) sts loosely.

Finishing

Join shoulder seams.
Set in sleeves placing any fullness evenly over top of sleeve cap. Sew side and sleeve seams in one line.

COLLAR/HOOD

Using circular needle, with RS facing and starting at right shoulder seam, pick up and knit 2 sts from holders at back neck edge, plus 1 extra st in between, 46 sts from holder at center back, 2 sts (plus 1 st in between) up other side back neck edge, 7 sts down vertical left front neck, 12 sts on hold along left neck edge, 26 sts from holder at center front, 12 sts on hold along right neck edge and 7 sts up to right shoulder seam. 116 sts.
Join in the round and work 20 in. (51cm) in st st (knit every round).
Bind off loosely to allow collar to roll along edge.

ALTERNATIVE SHORT COLLAR

As above until 116 sts are picked up. Then work 28 rows as above. Bind off loosely.

Regina

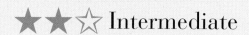

Simple stitches create the asymmetrical lines of this long chenille jacket—you can count on this elegant knit to keep you snug and cozy while walking the dog.

★ ★ ☆ Intermediate

SIZES

	XS	S	M	L	XL	
To fit bust	32	34	36	38	40	in.
	81	86	91	97	102	cm

See diagram on page 121 for actual measurements.

YARN

8 (9:10:11:12) × 3½ oz. (100g) balls of Sirdar Wow in Cobalt Blue 752

NOTIONS

1 large button or clasp
1 large press stud

NEEDLES

Pair each of US 10½ (6½mm) and US 11 (8mm) needles
US 10 (6mm) circular needle
US 11 (8mm) crochet hook

GAUGE

8 sts and 15 rows to 4 in. (10cm) measured over pattern using US 10½ (7mm) needles. Change needle size if necessary to obtain this gauge.

ABBREVIATIONS

See page 12.

STITCHES

Pattern 1 (for Back, Right Front and Left Sleeve)
  Row 1 (RS): *K3, p1, k2; rep from * to end.
  Row 2: Purl.
  Repeat these 2 rows.
Pattern 2 (for Left Front and Right Sleeve)
  Row 1 (RS): Knit.
  Row 2: Purl.
  Rows 3–10: Rep Rows 1 and 2 respectively.
  Row 11: Knit.
  Row 12: Knit.
  Repeat Rows 1–12.

Back

Using larger needles, cast on 34 (36:38:40:42) sts and knit 2 rows. Change to smaller needles and continue in Pattern 1 to end, centring pattern as follows:

XS K2, *k3, p1, k2; rep from * to last st, k2.
S *K3, p1, k2; rep from * to end.
M K1, *k3, p1, k2; rep from * to last st, k1.
L K2, *k3, p1, k2; rep from * to last 2 sts, k2.
XL *K3, p1, k2; rep from * to end.
Cont until work measures 17½ (17½:17:18:18) in. [44.5 (44.5:43:45.75:45.75)cm] from cast-on edge, ending on a WS row.

SHAPE ARMHOLE

Bind off 2 (2:2:3:3) sts at beg of next 2 rows. Then dec 1 st at both ends of next and every foll row 1 (2:2:2:3) times in all, keeping patt correct as set. 28 (28:30:30:30) sts. Cont until work measures 25 (25:25:26:26) in. [63.5 (63.5:63.5:66:66)cm] from cast-on edge, ending on a WS row.

SHAPE NECK AND SHOULDERS

Next row (RS): Work 9 sts, bind off 10 (10:12:12:12) sts loosely, join a second ball of yarn and work to end. Working both sides at the same time, work and place 5 sts on holder at armhole edge on next row (for left back neck it will be foll row), work to end of row. Using larger needles, bind off over all 9 sts.

Left Front

Using larger needles cast on 26 (28:30:32:34) sts and knit 2 rows. Change to smaller needles and work in Pattern 2 to end. Cont until work measures 17½ (17½:17:18:18) in. [44.5 (44.5:43:45.75:45.75)cm] from cast-on edge, ending on a WS row.

SHAPE ARMHOLE

Bind off 2 (2:2:3:3) sts at beg of next row. Work 1 row. Dec 1 st at armhole edge on next and every foll row 1 (2:2:2:3) times, keeping patt correct as set. 23 (24:26:27:28) sts. Cont until work measures

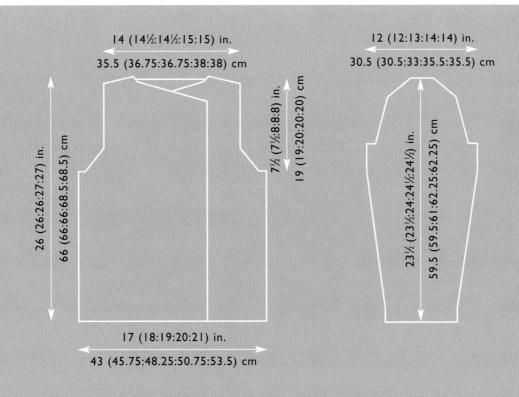

14 (14½:14½:15:15) in.
35.5 (36.75:36.75:38:38) cm

12 (12:13:14:14) in.
30.5 (30.5:33:35.5:35.5) cm

7½ (7½:8:8:8) in.
19 (19:20:20:20) cm

26 (26:26:27:27) in.
66 (66:66:68.5:68.5) cm

23½ (23½:24:24½:24½) in.
59.5 (59.5:61:62.25:62.25) cm

17 (18:19:20:21) in.
43 (45.75:48.25:50.75:53.5) cm

23½ (23½:23½:24½:24½) in.
[59.5 (59.5:59.5:62:62)cm] from cast-on edge, ending on a WS row.

SHAPE NECKLINE

Work to last 4 (5:5:6:6) sts, wrap next st (see page 96), turn and work next row. Work to last 5 (5:6:6:6) sts, wrap next st, turn and work next row. Work to last 5 (5:6:6:7) sts, wrap next st, turn and work next row. Work 1 row over all 23 (24:26:27:28) sts and then bind off 14 (15:17:18:19) sts at beg of next row, work to end.
Next row: Work and place 5 sts on holder, work to end. Using larger needles, bind off over all 9 sts.

Right Front

As Left Front, but refer to Pattern 1 after first 2 rows and repeat to end, reversing all shapings. Center patt as follows:
XS K2, *k3, p1, k2; rep from * to end.
S K2 *k3, p1, k2; rep from * to last 2 sts, k2.
M *K3, p1, k2; rep from * to end.
L K2, *k3, p1, k2; rep from * to last 2 sts, k2.
XL K2 *k3, p1, k2; rep from * to last 2 sts, k2.
Work buttonhole 2 rows before neck shaping as follows:
With WS facing, work to last 4 sts, bind off 2 sts, work to end. Cast on the 2 sts again when you come to them on next row.

Left Sleeve

Using larger needles, cast on 19 (19:20:20:20) sts and knit 2 rows. Change to smaller needles and cont in Pattern 1 to end, inc as follows:
XS, S, M, and L 1 st at both ends of Row 17, then foll 18th row twice. 25(25:26:26) sts.
XL 1 st at both ends of Row 13, then foll 14th row 3 times. 28 sts.

Incorporate all increased sts into patt.
Center patt as follows:
XS and S *K3, p1, k2; rep from * to last st, k1.
M, L and XL K1, *k3, p1, k2; rep from * to last st, k1.
Cont until work measures
17 (17½:18:18:18½) in. [43 (44.5:45.75:45.75:47)cm] from cast-on edge, ending on a WS row.

SHAPE SLEEVE CAP

Bind off 2 (2:2:3:3) sts at beg of next 2 rows. Then dec 1 st at both ends of next and every foll 4th row 0 (0:0:4:1) times, then every foll 3rd row 4 (4:4:2:6) times, then every foll alt row 4 (4:4:0:0) times, keeping patt correct as set. Using larger needles, bind off rem 5 (5:6:8:8) sts loosely.

Right Sleeve

As for Left Sleeve, but refer to Pattern 2 after first 2 rows and repeat to end.

Finishing

Use a small neat overcast stitch on very edge of work for all seams. Join shoulder seams. Set in sleeves, placing any fullness evenly across armhole. Join side and sleeve seams in one line, leaving bottom edge open for 4 in. (10cm). Using US 11 (8mm) crochet hook, starting at right center front neck edge, work 1 row of single crochet around neck edge.
Attach button to Left Front to correspond with buttonhole placing. Attach press-stud at top of Left Front on right side and corresponding place on wrong side of Right Front.

Elinor

Get the Hollywood touch with this diaphanous cape. Draped over the little black dress, it has classic appeal. For a weekend look, pair this stunning accessory with your favorite jeans.

 Intermediate

SIZES
One size

See diagram on page 125 for actual measurements.

YARN
4 x 1 oz. (25g) balls of Rowan Kidsilk Night in Moonlight 608

NEEDLES
Pair each of US 3 (3.25mm) and US 8 (5mm) needles
1 extra US 8 (5mm) needle
Stitch markers

GAUGE
22 sts and 28 rows to 4 in. (10cm) measured over stockinette stitch using US 8 (5mm) needles. Change needle size if necessary to obtain this gauge.

ABBREVIATIONS
See page 12.

STITCHES
Stockinette stitch
1 x 1 rib

Cape

Using larger needles, beginning at lower edge of cape, cast on 278 sts.
**Beg with knit row, work 13 rows st st, ending with knit row.
Row 14: Knit.
Row 15: Purl**.
Then work decreases as follows:
Dec row 1: K4, *k2tog, k10, k2tog, k2; repeat from * to last 18 sts, k2tog, k10, k2tog, k4. 244 sts.
Next row: Purl.
Next row: Knit.
Repeat from ** to ** once.
Dec row 2: K4, *k2tog, k8, k2tog, k2; repeat from * to last 16 sts, k2tog, k8, k2tog, k4. 210 sts.
Next row: Purl.
Next row: Knit.
Repeat from ** to ** once.
Dec row 3: K4, *k2tog, k6, k2tog, k2; repeat from * to last 14 sts, k2tog, k6, k2tog, k4. 176 sts.
Next row: Purl.
Next row: Knit.
Repeat from ** to ** once.
Dec row 4: K4, *k2tog, k4, k2tog, k2; repeat from * to last 12 sts, (k2tog, k4) twice. 142 sts.
Next row: Purl.
Next row: Knit.
Repeat from ** to ** once.
Dec row 5: K4, *k2tog, k2; repeat from * to last 6 sts, k2tog, k4. 108 sts.
Next row: Purl.

Next row: Knit.

Beg with knit row, work 13 rows st st, ending with knit row. Using double yarn for extra strength, bind off loosely purlwise.

Finishing

TIES (MAKE 2)

The wide purl stripes of cape are RS of work. With RS of work facing and smaller needles, pick up and k56 sts along one side edge.

Row 1: *K2tog, p1, k1, p2tog, k1, p1; rep from * to end of row. 42 sts.

Work 2 in. (5cm) in k1, p1 rib.

Leave on holder.

Using larger needles cast on 111 sts.

Row 1: Knit. Mark center 3 sts.

Row 2: K1, purl to center 3 sts, p3tog, purl to last st, k1.

Row 3: Knit.

Row 4: Knit to center 3 sts, k3tog, knit to end of row.

Row 5: K1, purl to last st, k1.

Row 6: Knit to center 3 sts, k3tog, knit to end of row.

Repeat Rows 1 to 6 three times more then Rows 1 to 4 once. 83 sts.

Divide these sts on two needles (41 and 42) having both points facing yarn.

THREE-NEEDLE BIND-OFF
This is a neat way of joining seams on inside, or decoratively on outside, especially if the shoulder shaping is short-rowed.

Place right sides together, back sts on one needle and front sts on another. *work 2 tog (1 from front needle and 1 from back needle). Rep from * once. Bind off first st over 2nd st. Cont to work 2 tog (1 front st and 1 back) and bind off across.

Fold work in half with RS facing (side with the 5 purl stripes is right side).

Bind off loosely with three needles (see "three-needle bind off" above), knitting tog 1 st from each needle to join piece down center. Using larger needles, with RS facing pick up 42 sts along straight edge. With RS facing, work three-needle bind-off as before on larger needles over 42 sts on holder and 42 sts of tie.

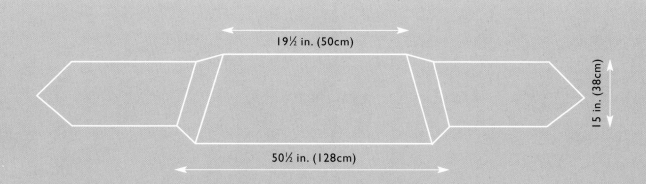

19½ in. (50cm)

50½ in. (128cm)

15 in. (38cm)

Sources and Resources

ARTESANO (UK & Worldwide)
Artesano Ltd.
28 Mansfield Road, Reading
Berkshire RG1 6AJ
+44 (0)118 9503350
Artesano is also the UK distributor of Brittany Needles
www.artesano.co.uk

DEBBIE BLISS (UK)
Designer Yarns
Units 8–10 Newbridge Industrial Estate
Pitt Street, Keighley
West Yorks BD21 4PQ
+44 (0)1535 664222
www.designeryarns.uk.com

DEBBIE BLISS (US)
Knitting Fever, Inc.
315 Bayview Ave.
Amityville, NY 11701
(516) 546-3600
www.knittingfever.com

LION BRAND YARN CO.
34 West 15th St.
New York, NY 10011
(212) 243-8995

ROWAN & JAEGER (UK)
Rowan
Green Lane Mill
Holmfirth
West Yorks HD9 2DX
+44 (0)1484 681881
www.knitrowan.com

ROWAN & JAEGER (US)
Westminster Fibers, Inc.
4 Townsend West Ste. 8
Nashua, NH 03063
(603) 886-5041 x 5043

ROWAN & JAEGER (Canada)
Diamond Yarn (Canada)
155 Martin Ross, Unit 3
Toronto M3J 2L9
Ontario
(416) 736-1111
www.diamondyarn.com

SIRDAR (UK)
Sirdar Spinning Limited
Flanshaw Lane
Alverthorpe
Wakefield
West Yorkshire
WF2 9ND
+44 (0)1924 371501
www.sirdar.co.uk

SIRDAR (US)
Knitting Fever, Inc.
315 Bayview Ave.
Amityville, NY 11701
(516) 546-3600
www.knittingfever.com

SIRDAR (Canada)
Diamond Yarn (Canada) Corp
155 Martin Ross
Unit 3
Toronto M3J 2L9
Ontario
(416) 736-6111
www.diamondyarn.com

*Knit kits and finished pieces for all designs
in this book can be ordered from:*

JEAN MOSS HANDKNITS
17 Clifton Dale
York YO30 6LJ
UK
Tel/fax: +44 (0)1904 646282
www.jeanmoss.com

Index

Acknowledgments

I'd like to thank everyone involved in producing *Contemporary Classics*—in particular all the talented knitters who produced the samples with very tight deadlines. So a big thank you to you all, but especially to Ann Banks, Jenny Poole, Glennis Garnett, Mary Coe, and Susan Armitage, who pulled out all the stops. Thanks also to: Rosemary Wilkinson for inviting me to work on the project. Clare Sayer for her meticulous editing. Sian Irvine for the photography and Isobel Gillan for the design. Tom Coomber of Artesano, David Watt of Designer Yarns, Kate Buller of Rowan, and David Rawson and Sue Batley-Kyle of Sirdar Yarns for their invaluable help in supporting this book and providing beautiful and inspiring yarns. Brittany for their super needles. Sandra Reston for her helpful and generous advice—her suggestions, though not always heeded, are as ever inspiring. Philip Mercer for his support and practical help in every area.